Conservation

WITHDRAWN

London: H M S O

Researched and written by Reference Services, Central Office of Information.

© Crown copyright 1993
Applications for reproduction should be made to HMSO.
First published 1993

ISBN 0 11 701726 4

HMSO publications are available from:

HMSO Publications Centre
(Mail, fax and telephone orders only)
PO Box 276, London SW8 5DT
Telephone orders 071-873 9090
General enquiries 071-873 0011
(queuing system in operation for both numbers)
Fax orders 071-873 8200

HMSO Bookshops
49 High Holborn, London WC1V 6HB   071-873 0011
Fax 071-873 8200 (counter service only)
258 Broad Street, Birmingham B1 2HE   021-643 3740   Fax 021-643 6510
Southey House, 33 Wine Street, Bristol BS1 2BQ
0272 264306   Fax 0272 294515
9-21 Princess Street, Manchester M60 8AS   061-834 7201   Fax 061-833 0634
16 Arthur Street, Belfast BT1 4GD   0232 238451   Fax 0232 235401
71 Lothian Road, Edinburgh EH3 9AZ   031-228 4181   Fax 031-229 2734

HMSO's Accredited Agents
(see Yellow Pages)

and through good booksellers

Contents

Acknowledgments

This book has been compiled with the co-operation of several organisations, including other government departments and agencies. The Central Office of Information would like to thank all those who have contributed their comments, and in particular: the Department of the Environment, the Department of National Heritage, the Ministry of Agriculture, Fisheries and Food, the Ministry of Defence, the Scottish Office, the Welsh Office, the Northern Ireland Office, English Heritage, English Nature, the Countryside Commission, the Countryside Council for Wales, Scottish Natural Heritage, the Forestry Commission, the Rural Development Commission, and the National Trust.

Photograph Credits

Numbers refer to the pages of the illustration section (2 to 8): Northern Ireland Tourist Board p.2 (top); Wales Tourist Board p.2 (bottom); Department of the Environment p.3 (top); Countryside Council for Wales p.3 (bottom) and p.5 (bottom); English Heritage p.5 (top) and p.6 (top); Tesco p.7 (top).

Introduction

Britain[1] has for many years had policies and laws designed to protect both its natural environment and built heritage. For example, the first Act of Parliament to protect old buildings, the Ancient Monuments Protection Act, was passed as long ago as 1882. Official bodies such as English Nature, English Heritage and their equivalents, and voluntary groups such as the National Trust, work hard to protect the national heritage. Britain is also involved in international conservation efforts and has signed important agreements with other countries to protect wildlife, habitats and heritage sites. A wide variety of designations are used to protect areas, sites and monuments that are of special interest to conservationists.

A very active voluntary sector supplements the efforts made by the Government. A wide variety of organisations work towards the conservation of differing aspects of Britain's national heritage. Many of these groups have very large memberships. Further information on developments in conservation is contained in *Current Affairs: A Monthly Survey*, published by HMSO.

---

[1]The term 'Britain' is used informally in this book to mean the United Kingdom of Great Britain and Northern Ireland. 'Great Britain' comprises England, Scotland and Wales.

Administration and Policies

Administrative Arrangements

The two principal departments concerned with conservation in England are the Department of the Environment and the Department of National Heritage. However, many of the government functions are performed by, or with the advice of, national agencies set up for that purpose. These include English Nature (see p. 18), the Countryside Commission (see p. 18), the Rural Development Commission (RDC—see p. 22) and English Heritage (see p. 47). There are also similar government bodies in Scotland and Wales.

Department of the Environment

Until April 1992, the Department of the Environment was the government department primarily responsible for conservation policies in England. It still retains important conservation functions, but some have been transferred to the new Department of National Heritage. Among the responsibilities retained by the Secretary of State for the Environment are:

—oversight of land use planning[2] including decisions on listed building consent;

—oversight of countryside and nature conservation policies;

—control of pollution; and

[2]For further details, see *Planning* (Aspects of Britain: HMSO, 1992).

—designation of areas of special conservation interest, such as Ramsar sites (see p. 12) or national nature reserves (see p. 26).

Department of National Heritage

A new government department, the Department of National Heritage,[3] was set up in April 1992 to handle, among other things, some aspects of the conservation of the built heritage. Among the functions that have been transferred to the Secretary of State for National Heritage are:

—listing buildings of special architectural or historic interest;

—scheduling ancient monuments to protect them from demolition or alteration (see p. 52) and making decisions on scheduled monument consent;

—upkeep of nationally-owned historical monuments, which is done through English Heritage;

—maintenance of the royal parks, which are open to the public, and royal palaces; and

—the protection of historic wrecks off the coast of England.

Wales, Scotland and Northern Ireland

Similar duties in Wales and Scotland are handled by the Secretaries of State for Wales and Scotland, with the help of Cadw and Historic Scotland (see p. 48) respectively. The Department of the Environment for Northern Ireland, part of the Northern Ireland Office, also has a very wide role in conservation matters in Northern Ireland. Conservation and related matters form an important part of the work of these departments, and large sums

[3]For further details, see *The British System of Government* (Aspects of Britain: HMSO, 1992).

are devoted to such purposes. For example, over £60 million has been made available in government grants since 1979 for the repair and maintenance of historic houses and churches in Scotland.

Other Departments

Other government departments also have a role in assisting the conservation of Britain's natural resources and built heritage.

The Ministry of Agriculture, Fisheries and Food is responsible for farming policies and related environmental and rural policies and programmes, for example, the Environmentally Sensitive Areas scheme (see p. 32). It is also responsible for fisheries policy. Britain conserves its fish stocks within the European Community's Common Fisheries Policy. Total allowable catch levels are set annually, based partly on independent scientific advice. The Ministry also has overall responsibility for coastal protection and flood defence; it requires authorities to consult the relevant environmental bodies about proposed works at an early stage, so that design decisions can take account of environmental interests. In Scotland, these responsibilities lie with the Scottish Office.

The Ministry of Defence holds a large number of sites used for military training. Because these include many areas that remain free from cultivation or urban development, the defence estate has considerable conservation value, containing over 200 Sites of Special Scientific Interest (SSSIs—see p. 27). The defence estate also includes important archaeological remains; there are more than 1,500 on Salisbury Plain alone, for which a marking and fencing programme to protect the most important is under way. Historic buildings in the care of the Ministry include Eltham Palace in south-east London, now the headquarters of the Royal Army Education Corps. The Ministry first appointed a conservation officer in the mid-1970s, and since then a network of some 200 conservation groups has grown up to work with the Ministry. In February 1992, the Ministry of Defence reaffirmed its commitment to environmental conservation by signing a declaration of intent with English Nature. This will ensure the continuation of conservation initiatives agreed with the former Nature Conservancy Council. The agreement provides for close consultation on the management of important sites within the defence estate and for careful planning on their usage and disposal.

This Common Inheritance

In September 1990 the Government published a White Paper on the environment, *This Common Inheritance*, which sets out the Government's intentions for strengthening its policies on conservation and environmental protection. It spelled out over 350 separate actions that the Government intended to take, many of them relating to conservation. Among the commitments in the White Paper were:

—a campaign to advise farmers how to protect their countryside assets;

—continued encouragement for environmentally sensitive tree planting through existing grant schemes;

—support for the development of new forestry initiatives;

—an examination of the scope to recreate habitats affected by road schemes;

—government endorsement of the Countryside Commission's target to put the right-of-way network in good order by the year 2000;

—a review of the operation of the Environmentally Sensitive Areas scheme;

—work towards better arrangements for common land management and access;

—work towards designating more marine nature reserves, and consideration of the extension of the marine consultation area scheme from Scotland to the rest of Britain;

—continued funding for the building programme for national museums and galleries;

—work to promote the educational value of historic sites;

—continued tax reliefs and grants to support the built heritage;

—more emphasis within the grants system for buildings in towns and the industrial heritage;

—government grants to help cathedrals;

—complete resurveys of the country's heritage sites;

—the transfer of responsibility for historic wrecks to join that for archaeology on land; and

—improved protection for ancient monuments.

Many of these specific actions have already been implemented.

A follow-up report, *This Common Inheritance: the First Year Report*, was published in September 1991. As well as charting progress on the commitments contained in the original White Paper, it set out over 400 new actions that the Government proposed to take. These included:

—the publication of guidelines on community woodland design and forest recreation;

—the launching of woodland management grants under the Woodland Grant Scheme;

—the production of a green tourism manual to give guidance on how tourism can help the rural economy with the least damage to the environment;

—development of the Countryside Stewardship scheme (see p. 34);

—the issue of new planning guidance on nature conservation; and

—work towards the signature by the end of 1992 of a new agreement between the Baltic and North Sea states on site and species protection.

A further follow-up report was published in October 1992. Among the commitments in this paper were to:

—issue a final planning policy guidance note on nature conservation (see p. 21) by the end of 1992;

—review the effectiveness of Green Belts (see p. 33) in the light of research;

—legislate for better common land arrangements when parliamentary time allows;

—publish guidelines for the management of all semi-natural woodland types by the end of 1992;

—set up an advisory panel on native woodlands in the Scottish Highlands in autumn 1992; and

—re-examine building listing policy in the light of the present resurvey.

Action for the Countryside

In February 1992, the Government announced the *Action for the Countryside* initiative, a statement of policies for the countryside developed in co-operation by the Department of the Environment, the Ministry of Agriculture, Fisheries and Food, the Countryside Commission, English Nature, the Forestry Commission and the RDC. It includes a package of new and extended conservation and improvement measures. These include:

—draft government guidance for local authorities on development policies consistent with nature conservation;

—draft guidance on preparing strategies for the creation of new forests and woodlands (see p. 38);

—a pilot scheme in selected rural areas to stimulate the economy and deal with problems arising from agricultural change, administered by the RDC;

—a scheme to encourage improved management of valued hedgerows;

—an initiative to assist in improving the rights-of-way network;

—a scheme to promote wildlife conservation by paying for positive management of SSSIs;

—a programme to enhance the abundance and distribution of scarce and vulnerable species;

—a scheme to assist parish-level action to improve the environment; and

—increased financial incentives to encourage the planting of woodland on farms.

In March 1992 the Government issued a consultation document in Scotland entitled *The Scottish Office Rural Framework*. It provides a context within which rural policy in Scotland might develop, and sets out several themes to promote discussion on shifting the emphasis towards a more integrated approach. It offers government departments and agencies and local authorities the freedom to pursue their own specific objectives within a common policy framework.

Millennium Fund

The Government intends to establish a Millennium Fund, subject to parliamentary approval. This would be supported by the proceeds of the proposed national lottery. Among the things which the Millennium Fund could support are:

—the restoration of the buildings that symbolise and enrich British life;

—help for local communities and voluntary groups to run their own Millennium projects for local restoration schemes; and

—Millennium bursaries for young or newly-retired people offering their time to schemes designed to change the face of Britain by the year 2000.

International Bodies and Agreements

Britain is a member of many international bodies which have a bearing on conservation. Among these is the United Nations Environment Programme, to which Britain is contributing £4.5 million in 1992–93.

Britain has also signed many treaties and conventions to protect wildlife and preserve important sites, as well as joining international bodies that provide forums for discussion of transnational conservation issues. Important initiatives include:

—the Berne Convention on the Conservation of European Wildlife and Natural Habitats;

—the Ramsar Convention on Wetlands of International Importance;

—the Bonn Convention on the Conservation of Migratory Species of Wild Animals;

—the Convention on International Trade in Endangered Species of Wild Fauna and Flora (CITES); and

—the World Heritage Convention, drawn up in 1972, which aims to secure lasting protection for sites of great international significance.

International Treaties

UNCED Meeting

Britain supports the work of the World Commission on Environment and Development, which in 1987 produced *Our Common Future*, known as the Brundtland Report, on sustainable development. The concept of sustainable development was taken forward at the United Nations Conference on Environment and Development, popularly known as the 'Earth Summit', which met in Rio de Janeiro, Brazil, from 3 to 14 June 1992. A number of important initiatives were agreed at this meeting, including a framework convention on climate change and a convention on the protection of biological diversity. Britain will publish its national action plan for the implementation of the latter and has offered to host the first meeting of parties to the convention. The meeting also agreed Agenda 21, an action framework for the twenty-first century, a declaration setting out clear principles for sustainable development, and a declaration for the management of forests. Britain announced the establishment of the Darwin Initiative for the Survival of Species, which will build on Britain's recognised scientific and commercial strength to:

—involve international studies of natural resources;

—help set goals for research;

—build up an inventory of the most important species and habitats; and

—help all countries to exchange skills and information.

Berne Convention

The Berne Convention was ratified by Britain in 1982. Its aim is to protect wild flora and fauna in their natural habitats, especially where conservation requires the co-operation of several states.

Ramsar Convention

The Ramsar Convention was signed in 1971 to protect wetlands of international importance. Under this, some 57 sites in Britain have been designated for protection. Other sites are under consideration for inclusion.

Bonn Convention

Britain is one of 39 parties to the Bonn Convention, which was signed in 1979 and protects migratory animals. Agreements have been made under the Convention to protect specific species or groups of animals. For example, in May 1992, Britain was one of the first countries to sign an agreement under the Bonn Convention to conserve dolphins and other small cetaceans in the Baltic and North Seas. Under this agreement, international co-operation both in research and management will be ensured.

Convention on International Trade in Endangered Species

Britain strongly supports the work of CITES, the international agreement under which the trade in products from endangered species of flora and fauna is controlled. Many species are protected by an absolute ban on trade; for example, leopards, cheetahs and rhinoceroses. African elephants are also protected by a prohibition of trade in ivory and other products. At the eighth meeting of CITES in Kyoto, Japan, in March 1992, Britain successfully opposed proposals to downlist certain populations of these species so as to allow controlled trade in their products. Britain also played a leading role in moves to impose new curbs on trade in wildlife, particularly the trade in wild birds. The measures agreed will:

—improve consultation with exporting countries where doubts exist about the sustainability of trade in particular species;

—establish machinery for stringent action, such as trade bans, on trade being conducted at unsustainable levels;

—provide for the suspension of trade in bird species subject to high mortality in transport; and

—improve the provision of scientific information about the mortality of wild-caught birds.

World Heritage Convention

The World Heritage List has been drawn up under the United Nations Educational, Scientific and Cultural Organisation's World Heritage Convention to identify and protect sites of outstanding universal value. There are already 13 entries for Britain, and other sites may be added in due course. Sites so far included are:

—Canterbury Cathedral, with St Augustine's Abbey and St Martin's Church in Kent;

—Durham Cathedral and Castle;

—Studley Royal Gardens and Fountains Abbey in North Yorkshire;

—Ironbridge Gorge, with the world's first iron bridge and other early industrial sites, in Shropshire;

—the prehistoric stone circles at Stonehenge and Avebury in Wiltshire;

—Blenheim Palace in Oxfordshire;

—the city of Bath in Avon;

—Hadrian's Wall;

—the Tower of London;

—the Palace of Westminster, Westminster Abbey and St Margaret's, Westminster, also in London;

—the St Kilda islands in Scotland;

—the castles and town walls of King Edward I in north Wales; and

—the Giant's Causeway and Causeway Coast in Northern Ireland.

Government support for these sites can be considerable. For example, in 1991 a £4 million endowment for the Ironbridge Heritage Foundation was announced. This will ensure a secure future for these remains of the earliest days of the Industrial Revolution.

European Community

The European Community (EC) also plays an important role in conservation. For example, 55 sites in Britain, covering over 157,000 hectares (390,000 acres), have been designated as Special Protection Areas under an EC directive on the conservation of wild birds, with other sites under consideration. Britain is continuing to designate suitable sites for protection. For example, in March 1992 the Exe estuary, Old Hall Marshes (Essex) and part of Lindisfarne (Northumberland) were designated as both Special Protection Areas and Ramsar sites, and Chippenham Fen (Cambridgeshire) was also listed as a Ramsar site. About 175 further sites are being considered for Special Protection Area status and over 130 for Ramsar listing.

In May 1992 the Community adopted a directive on wildlife habitats, which will give a European dimension to the protection of sites important for wildlife. The directive identifies a range of habitat types which require protection on a European scale; those occurring in Britain include estuaries, species-rich grass and heathlands, bogs, coastal dunes and woodlands. Under the terms of the directive, a network of sites of Special Areas of Conservation for rare, endangered and vulnerable habitats and species will be established across the EC. This network will be known as Natura 2000. In Britain, the majority of these sites of international importance are likely to be drawn from the existing network of SSSIs.

The EC has also taken separate action to protect other species by imposing bans on the import of various animal products, for example, harp and hooded seal pup skins and whale products.

The reform of the Community's Common Agricultural Policy (CAP) was agreed in May 1992. This included a requirement for all member states to implement a series of measures to offer farmers incentives for managing their land in ways designed to offer environmental and nature conservation benefits.

Under the 1989 version of the Lomé Convention, an aid and trade agreement between the EC and developing countries, the environmental effects of a proposed development project must be taken into account before it is agreed.

Britain participates in the Biogenetic Reserve network established by the Council of Europe, which aims to conserve representative examples of European flora, fauna and natural areas, and to encourage biological research. A total of 18 sites in Britain are included in the network: seven dry grassland sites and 11 heathland sites. These sites were all put forward after successful consultations with the owners of the land concerned.

International Whaling Commission

Britain is a member of the International Whaling Commission (IWC), which imposed a moratorium on commercial whaling in 1982 to take effect from the 1985–86 hunting season. In the 1992 annual meeting, Britain successfully defended the continuation of the moratorium, and condemned the intention of some nations to resume commercial whaling. The Government made it clear that it would not contemplate any lifting of the moratorium unless it was satisfied on a number of points: that whale stocks were at healthy levels; that revised management procedures were robust, comprehensive, defensible and above all prudent; and that improvements were made in the present methods of killing whales to make them more humane. Other achievements at the 1992 meeting included:

— the adoption of a new British proposal on research into Antarctic ecosystems and the impact of the global environment on whale stocks;

— the strong endorsement by Britain of resolutions to study the establishment of a circumpolar whale sanctuary so that it could be adopted at the next annual meeting of the IWC;

— a successful resolution, co-sponsored by Britain, securing a whale sanctuary in the Indian Ocean for a further ten-year period; and

— the agreement of an 11-point action plan on humane killing methods, calling for regular reviews on methods and analysis of the times to death.

North Sea Conference

The countries around the North Sea have met in a series of North Sea Conferences to discuss measures to protect the marine environment. The third conference was held in The Hague, Netherlands, in March 1990. Most of the measures agreed were on the control and reduction of pollution, but matters relating directly to the conservation of wildlife were also agreed, including, as a result of a British initiative, action to protect dolphins and porpoises. Britain, which applies the measures agreed at the North Sea Conference to all its coastal waters, was the first of the participating countries to prepare a detailed action plan on its implementation programme; this was published in July 1990. A North Sea Task Force is preparing a report on environmental quality as a basis for the next conference in 1995.

Britain's Aid Programme

Britain helps the developing countries to conserve their environments. Its overseas aid programme, carried out by the Overseas Development Administration, includes:

—helping tropical countries with their forest management;

—promoting training in conservation-related skills;

—supporting wildlife parks to protect the diversity of life; and

—assisting individual projects to protect threatened species.

The Natural Heritage

Government Bodies

Britain protects its natural heritage and promotes access to the countryside through several government organisations, as well as by many voluntary sector groups (see pp. 62–78). The government bodies have various different roles, and they have recently been reorganised.

Reorganisation of Government Bodies

Until April 1991, the main government body responsible for nature conservation was the Nature Conservancy Council (NCC), whose remit covered all of Great Britain. The Countryside Commission and a separate Countryside Commission for Scotland (CCS) were responsible for countryside policy and promoting access to the countryside for recreation.

In April 1991, the NCC was replaced by separate agencies for England (English Nature), Scotland (the Nature Conservancy Council for Scotland—NCCS) and Wales (the Countryside Council for Wales—CCW). The CCW has also taken over from the Countryside Commission in Wales, leaving the Commission responsible for countryside policy in England only. A Joint Nature Conservation Committee (JNCC), which is a statutory committee established by the three nature conservation councils and includes representatives from all three, the Countryside Commission, and from Northern Ireland under an independent chairman, was established to advise the Government on matters of national and international importance.

Another alteration—which had been proposed at the same time as the other change—took place in April 1992. The two Scottish bodies—the CCS and the NCCS—merged to form a single body, Scottish Natural Heritage (SNH). The Government believes that bringing the two bodies together will offer the chance to promote co-operation in the conservation and sustainable development of Scotland's natural resources and end the duplication of effort caused by having two separate agencies, both concerned with closely allied issues.

The Government supports the work of the nature conservation and countryside organisations with a considerable amount of money. For 1992–93, grants-in-aid have been allocated of over £36 million for English Nature, £38 million for the Countryside Commission, nearly £35 million for SNH and £17 million for the CCW. The JNCC budget of £5 million is jointly funded by the three nature conservation councils. An additional £1.04 million government help for English Nature was announced in October 1992, aimed at safeguarding important peatland sites, supplementing expenditure on management agreements and to meet an accelerated programme to designate SPAs under the European Community birds directive.

Nature Conservation Bodies
The work that these bodies do is large and varied in its scope. The nature conservation bodies are, among other things, responsible for:

—establishing, maintaining and managing national nature reserves and marine nature reserves;

—identifying and notifying SSSIs;

—providing grants for nature conservation;

—providing advice and information about nature conservation;

—supporting and conducting research; and

—advising the Government on relevant nature conservation matters.

The nature conservation councils can make financial support available to help other groups' conservation projects. For example, in 1991 English Nature made a grant of £12,500 to a project designed to increase the distribution and protection of otters in Yorkshire, Lancashire and Cumbria. In 1992 the CCW supported ten land purchases by voluntary bodies. For example, the Gwent Wildlife Trust was helped to buy Pentwyn Farm, a farmstead with four traditionally managed haymeadows.

As well as declaring national nature reserves, the nature conservation agencies can enter into management agreements with the owners and occupiers of SSSIs to help them manage their land to benefit nature conservation. In 1991–92 over £5.7 million was spent on such agreements in England alone. The agencies can also sign statements of intent with large landholders—for example, the Ministry of Defence.

Advice on nature conservation is provided not only to the Government, but also to other people, such as industry, farmers, voluntary conservation organisations and members of the public. In particular, the nature conservation bodies have an advisory role in the planning system. Local planning authorities have to consult the relevant nature conservation body during the preparation of development plans.[4] They must also consult them when consider-

[4]For further details, see *Planning* (Aspects of Britain: HMSO, 1992).

ing planning applications that fall within the boundaries of SSSIs. In England and Wales, this duty was extended in January 1992 so that the relevant body also has to be consulted about applications outside an SSSI but likely to affect it. New government guidance is being prepared on nature conservation in relation to the planning system, as promised in *This Common Inheritance*. The draft version of this guidance was published for consultation in February 1992; it looks to local planning authorities to take account of nature conservation interests wherever these are relevant to local planning decisions.

The nature conservation bodies undertake a considerable amount of research. For example, in 1986 the former NCC set up a comprehensive long-term research programme to analyse the actual and potential damage to plants and animals caused by pesticide spraying; this work is being continued by English Nature. In 1991–92 English Nature managed 45 research projects with a total value of £795,000. The CCW devoted £800,000 to its research projects in 1991–92.

Joint Nature Conservation Committee

The primary purpose of the JNCC is to maintain and strengthen the national and international perspective on nature conservation. Among other things, it:

—sets the standards and criteria by which the national bodies work in notifying SSSIs; and

—advises the Government on Britain's international obligations.

For example, it provided advice to the Government during the negotiations on the EC's habitats directive. The JNCC also undertakes research on behalf of its supporting bodies and sets standards for surveying and monitoring. Its work is supported by its own specialist staff, who are seconded from the three nature conservation agencies.

Countryside Agencies

In England, the Countryside Commission promotes the enjoyment of the countryside; in Scotland and Wales these functions fall to SNH and the CCW in addition to their nature conservation role. In England, the RDC promotes a healthy rural economy. The tasks of the countryside bodies include:

—conserving and enhancing the natural beauty of the countryside;

—encouraging the provision and improvement of facilities for open-air recreation;

—designating, subject to ministerial confirmation, National Parks and areas of outstanding natural beauty (AONBs) in England and Wales, and national scenic areas and natural heritage areas in Scotland;

—providing advice on the conservation and enjoyment of the countryside to the Government and other public bodies whose activities affect it;

—providing grant aid to landowners, farmers, local authorities and others to take action on conservation and recreation provision; and

—operating a range of economic and social programmes to assist the rural economy.

The countryside bodies promote farming and land management practices that are sensitive to the country landscape. A large number of farms have applied for payments to secure extra environmental and recreational benefits since the CAP set-aside scheme was established in 1989. The Countryside Commission was responsible, in conjunction with other bodies, for designing the Government's Countryside Stewardship scheme, which was launched in 1991. Recreational woodland is also being promoted by means of new community forests and a national forest.

As with the nature conservation bodies, the countryside bodies also advise on planning. For example, they are consulted on the preparation of development plans in England and Wales. Representations are also made on individual planning decisions.

The countryside bodies provide support for the countryside rangers appointed to help the public enjoy National Parks, AONBs and other sites. The Countryside Commission currently supports some 236 posts at over 100 sites. The CCW supports almost 200 posts. To encourage the recreational use of the countryside, a large number of country parks have been established—open spaces suitable for family recreation and situated within reasonable driving distance of large cities. They have car parks, tea rooms, facilities for disabled visitors and, in some cases, playgrounds.

Other Government Bodies

Besides the Countryside Commission, the RDC, English Nature and their parallel agencies, other bodies have an important part to play in the enjoyment and protection of the natural environment in Britain, including:

—the National Rivers Authority (NRA), which is responsible in England and Wales for, among other things, the water quality of rivers and lakes, and for inland fisheries;

—the Forestry Commission, which is the government department responsible for forestry; and

—the Natural Environment Research Council (NERC), which is a government body funding scientific research into the environment.

The NRA protects water quality, principally through the regulation of all effluent discharges into rivers and other inland waters (except those potentially most harmful, which are subject to the new system of integrated pollution control—IPC—and are controlled instead by Her Majesty's Inspectorate of Pollution—HMIP). Discharge consents issued by the NRA specify what may be discharged and set limits on the volume and content of effluent, in order to achieve appropriate water quality standards. The NRA maintains public registers containing information about discharge consents and water quality. The Government proposes to merge the functions of the NRA with those of HMIP into a unified Environment Agency. Similar arrangements to protect water quality apply in Scotland, where control is generally exercised by river purification authorities. The most potentially harmful wastes are subject to IPC, which is enforced by Her Majesty's Industrial Pollution Inspectorate or the relevant river purification authority. The proposed Scottish Environment Protection Agency would combine these enforcement agencies. The Department of the Environment for Northern Ireland is responsible for controlling water pollution in Northern Ireland. As a result of these measures, water quality in Britain's rivers is good, with 95 per cent of river, stream and canal lengths being good or fair, compared with 75 per cent in the EC generally.

The Forestry Commission is the national forestry authority in Great Britain, and gives the Government advice on forestry matters. A reorganisation in 1992 divided it into two sections, one with responsibility for its regulatory functions, while the other runs its own timber production. Its policy objectives include landscape amenity and environmental protection. An example of a Forestry Commission project to help wildlife conservation is the restoration of 140 hectares (350 acres) of heathland at Whitesheet in Dorset, announced in April 1991. Species of animal that will benefit from the removal of trees to join up several small heaths include smooth snakes, sand lizards, nightjars, woodlarks and the silver studded blue butterfly. The Commission has established 14 forest parks in Great Britain; these are large areas of forest, often with fine areas of mountain and other open country, where special provision has been made for public access and enjoyment. The Commission makes available advice on the environmental aspects of planting schemes through its publications, covering such matters as nature conservation and sites of archaeological importance. It is financed partly by the Government and partly by other income, such as the sale of timber. In Northern Ireland, the Department of Agriculture may acquire land for afforestation and give financial assistance for private planting.

The NERC has a science budget allocation of £130 million in 1992–93, plus expected receipts of about £43 million from commissioned research and other income. Established in 1965, it undertakes and supports research in the environmental sciences and funds postgraduate training. Its programmes encompass the marine, earth, terrestrial, freshwater, polar and atmospheric sciences. The NERC stresses international collaborative work on global environmental issues. However, it also does work of direct importance for wildlife conservation at home, for example in monitoring populations of seals in Britain's coastal waters (see p. 44).

Protection for the Countryside

Britain has a large number of policies and initiatives designed to protect the countryside. These include statutory status and recognition under the planning system for important areas.

Nature Reserves

There are 242 national nature reserves (NNRs) in Great Britain, which cover between them some 168,100 hectares (415,200 acres). They are established to protect the most important areas of natural or semi-natural vegetation and their flora and fauna. NNRs are protected by by-laws. Some are owned by English Nature or its equivalents, but others are managed by one of these bodies under a suitable agreement or by a voluntary body. There are 44 NNRs in Northern Ireland, either owned or leased by the Department of the Environment for Northern Ireland or managed in agreement with the owner. They cover some 4,400 hectares (10,900 acres).

In addition to the NNRs, there are many more reserves that are owned and managed by voluntary organisations—for example, over 2,000 reserves, totalling some 52,000 hectares (128,000 acres), belong to the local conservation trusts in the Royal Society for Nature Conservation (see p. 70).

The island of Lundy, off the coast of Devon, was declared as Britain's first marine nature reserve (MNR) in 1986. A second such reserve, Skomer (off the coast of Dyfed), was designated in 1990. Within an MNR, activities are regulated by a combination of national by-laws set by the nature conservation bodies, local by-laws and a voluntary code of conduct. Two more sites are under consideration to be designated as MNRs—Menai Strait and Bardsey and the Llŷn peninsula in Gwynedd.

Marine Consultation Areas

A government scheme to extend 'marine consultation areas' beyond Scotland was announced in February 1992. It proposes the designation of 16 sites in England and Wales as marine consultation areas, and has issued draft guidelines on procedures to be adopted. Under this scheme, all bodies taking decisions that might affect the conservation interest of the listed sites would be asked to consult English Nature or the CCW. Any advice given by the conservation agencies should be given due weight by decision-makers, and the conservation agencies should be informed of decisions taken. The scheme would be monitored by the JNCC, and annual reports would be made available to the public.

Sites of Special Scientific Interest

There are some 5,700 SSSIs in Great Britain, areas which have been designated for their plants, animal life or geological features. For example, Richmond Park in south-west London was notified as an SSSI in March 1992, the first Royal Park to be designated. Having been managed as a deer park since it was first enclosed by Charles I well over three centuries ago, it retains many important wildlife features. These include ancient trees and a rare group of beetles. Management objectives have been agreed between English Nature and the Department of the Environment, which at that time was responsible for the upkeep of the Royal Parks. The total area of SSSIs in Great Britain rose from 13,600 sq km (5,300 sq miles) in 1981 to 17,800 (6,900 sq miles) in 1991. In Northern Ireland, 36 Areas of Special Scientific Interest have been declared.

Most SSSIs are in private ownership. An area is notified as an SSSI by English Nature or its equivalent under the Wildlife and Countryside Act 1981. Once an area has been notified as an SSSI,

English Nature or its equivalent must be consulted before the occupier carries out any operation listed in the notification that might damage the SSSI. It might then suggest an alternative approach, which might be as simple as proposing a different date for hay cutting, or else persuade the owner or occupier not to go ahead and instead offer payment under a management agreement. English Nature had some 1,600 management agreements covering SSSIs in 1991–92. If the owners fail to consult properly before carrying out a damaging operation, they can be fined up to £1,000. Planning authorities are required to consult the relevant nature conservation body about planning applications for land in an SSSI or likely to affect it.

Out of the 5,700 SSSIs, damage was reported to 254 sites in 1990–91. However, in 218 of these cases—some 86 per cent of the total—this damage was considered to be short-term, and it was expected that the special interest would recover.

National Parks and Areas of Outstanding Natural Beauty

Areas of outstanding countryside can be protected by special designation as National Parks or AONBs or, in Scotland, as national scenic areas (NSAs).

There are ten National Parks in England and Wales:

—Brecon Beacons;

—Dartmoor;

—Exmoor;

—Lake District;

—North York Moors;

—Northumberland;

—Peak District;

—Pembrokeshire Coast;

—Snowdonia; and

—Yorkshire Dales.

Table 1: National Parks and Other Designated Areas, March 1991

	National Parks		Areas of Outstanding Natural Beauty[a]	
	Area (sq km)	Percentage of total area in region	Area (sq km)	Percentage of total area in region
England	9,838	7.0	18,979	14.5
Wales	4,098	20.0	715	3.5
Scotland	–	–	10,173	13.0
Northern Ireland	–	–	2,849	20.0

Sources: Countryside Commission, Countryside Commission for Scotland, Department of the Environment for Northern Ireland.

[a] NSAs in Scotland.

The National Parks aim to provide protection for the outstanding countryside in the parks and opportunities for outdoor recreation. The Parks are national in the sense that they are valuable to the nation as a whole, but most of the land is in private hands. Central government funding for National Parks rose to nearly £16 million in 1991–92. This is provided in the form of National Park Supplementary Grant, which meets 75 per cent of the Parks' approved expenditure. The remainder is provided by the county councils covering each Park's area.

Each National Park is responsible for various tasks, including:

—encouraging farmers to manage their land in suitable ways;

—employing park rangers;

—looking after rights of way;

—dealing with applications for planning permission for new developments in their areas (within which tighter planning controls apply); and

—providing information and educational material.

The Government is proposing the reform of the National Park authorities, so that they are all established as independent bodies—at present, only two, Lake District and Peak District, are. New National Parks can be designated by the Countryside Commission or the CCW, subject to confirmation from the relevant Secretary of State.

The Norfolk Broads are a unique tract of lakes and rivers in East Anglia, a very popular area for boating holidays. The Broads have not been designated as a National Park, but are managed along very similar lines and have equivalent protection. A special body, the Broads Authority, has been set up to administer the area. Its work includes projects such as an experimental programme of dredging to improve water quality in broads badly affected by silting, and management of the fens to encourage wildlife and scenery typical of the Broads. In January 1992 the Government announced that it intended that the New Forest in Hampshire should also receive statutory status and protection equivalent to that of a

National Park, subject to parliamentary approval. Like the Broads, it would have its own independent authority.

There are 39 AONBs in England and Wales, totalling about 20,400 sq km (7,900 sq miles). These differ from National Parks in lacking extensive tracts of open country suitable for recreation, but still have important landscape qualities. There are no special administrative arrangements for AONBs, but the Government encourages local councils to establish appropriate management arrangements and give them special attention in their planning work. There are nine AONBs in Northern Ireland, totalling about 2,800 sq km (1,100 sq miles).

National Scenic Areas and Natural Heritage Areas

There are 40 NSAs in Scotland, covering 10,200 sq km (3,900 sq miles), designated by the Secretary of State for Scotland. The local authorities retain responsibility for development control within these areas, but SNH is involved in certain classes of application. Local authorities are also responsible for drawing up suitable land-scape conservation policies in their structure and local plans. Working parties have been established to make recommendations for the management of Loch Lomond and the Trossachs, and the Cairngorms, two areas of considerable conservation value in Scotland.

Under the Scottish Natural Heritage Act 1991, which set up SNH, the Government also made provision for the designation of 'natural heritage areas' (NHAs) in Scotland. These would be designated by the Secretary of State for Scotland on the advice of SNH. Before designating an NHA, the Secretary of State will consult publicly on the proposals.

Once designated, an NHA will create a general framework within which the outstanding natural heritage importance of an area can be recognised by sensitive and sustainable management. The economic and social aspirations of local communities, and the desire for public access, are also regarded as important. Land managers within an NHA will be encouraged to adopt land use practices which are compatible with the overall aims of that NHA's management statement. All public agencies will be expected to take account of the broad aims of the NHA, and where appropriate will help prepare the management statement. Local planning authorities will also be expected to play a full role in this, and to take account of the views of SNH in drawing up or amending statutory development plans for the area.

Environmentally Sensitive Areas

Areas can also be declared as Environmentally Sensitive Areas (ESAs) by the agriculture departments. These are areas where the landscape or wildlife are of particular importance, and are vulnerable to more intensive farming. Incentive payments are made to farmers who maintain traditional farming practices. There are 19 ESAs in Britain, covering 387,000 hectares (⁻6,000 acres); since the needs of each vary, different practices may be required of the farmers in each area. In November 1991 the Government announced the creation of 12 new ESAs in England, to come into force in 1992–93, bringing the area covered in England to more than 1 million hectares (2.47 million acres). Further ESAs in Scotland, Wales and Northern Ireland have also been announced.

Heritage Coasts

Some 1,500 km (950 miles) of coastline along 45 stretches in England and Wales have been defined as 'Heritage Coasts' since the early 1970s. The aims of this designation were to conserve the natural beauty of the coastline and facilitate recreational use consistent with that. More recently, the Countryside Commission has reviewed these objectives and proposed that they should be widened to recognise the need to preserve and enhance important habitats for flora and fauna and to protect architectural, historical and archaeological features. The Government has welcomed these proposals. Many Heritage Coasts are afforded extra protection through other designations, for example, as National Parks, AONBs, SSSIs or Special Protection Areas under the EC Birds Directive. About a third of the designated length of Heritage Coast has been taken into the ownership of the National Trust (see p. 62), in recent years mostly through its Enterprise Neptune scheme.

In Scotland, 26 Preferred Coastal Conservation Zones have been defined. Their total length of 7,500 km (4,700 miles) covers 74 per cent of Scotland's mainland and island coastlines. Safeguards for these coasts are included in local plans.

Green Belts

The countryside outside several of Britain's major cities, including London, Birmingham, Edinburgh, Glasgow, Liverpool and Bristol, is protected by 'Green Belts', areas where it is intended that the land should be left open and free from inappropriate development. Their purpose is to:

—restrict the sprawl of large built-up areas;

—safeguard the surrounding countryside;

—stop neighbouring towns merging;

—preserve the special character of historic towns; and

—assist in urban regeneration.

They also have a recreational role. Some 1.5 million hectares (3.7 millions acres) in England and 145,000 hectares (360,000 acres) in Scotland are designated as Green Belt.

Countryside Stewardship

A pilot Countryside Stewardship scheme was launched in June 1991, which will cost over £25 million over the period 1992–93 to 1994–95. The scheme provides government funding to landowners and farmers to protect and enhance valued landscapes and habitats throughout England and enhance opportunities for the public to enjoy them. Typical annual payments range from £20 a hectare for managing lowland heath to £275 a hectare for creating riverside meadows and opening them for people to enjoy. Initially the scheme targeted chalk and limestone grasslands, heathland, waterside landscapes, coastal lands and upland areas, but in June 1992 it was extended to cover historic landscapes, including orchards, and old meadows and pastures.

The CCW launched its own experimental farmland stewardship scheme for Wales in July 1992. Tir Cymen offers farmers annual payments in return for the positive management of their land for the benefit of wildlife, landscape, archaeology and geology, and for providing new opportunities for the quiet enjoyment of the countryside. Similar levels of payment to Countryside Stewardship are anticipated.

Tree Protection

The felling of trees is regulated through a system of licence controls regulated by the Forestry Commission. In addition, local authorities can place 'tree preservation orders' on trees and woodland which they consider make an important contribution to amenity; it is in general an offence deliberately to fell or damage trees in contravention of a tree preservation order. There is also a duty on local authorities to consider when granting planning permission whether it is appropriate to impose conditions to protect existing trees or require new trees to be planted. The Government is undertaking a comprehensive review of tree preservation policies and legislation.

Hedgerows

A survey of hedgerow stock was carried out in 1990. This showed that there was a total length of 371,000 km (230,000 miles) of hedgerow in England and Wales, down from 410,000 km (255,000 miles) in 1984. In order to curb such losses of key hedgerows, the Government announced plans in *This Common Inheritance* to protect hedgerows. The Government's detailed proposals to protect hedgerows were published in July 1991. They included new arrangements which would require landowners to notify local planning authorities of intended removal, together with a power for local authorities to register such hedgerows to ensure their retention. A Private Member's Bill to implement this is receiving government support in Parliament.

A new hedgerow incentive scheme was launched in July 1992, to be administered by the Countryside Commission and developed in close co-operation with the Ministry of Agriculture, Fisheries and Food. Payments will be offered to farmers who restore and manage hedgerows in ways which will ensure their continued contribution to the landscape and to wildlife. The Government has allocated £3.5 million over three years to the scheme.

Derelict Land

In June 1991 the Government broadened the scope of its existing policies on derelict land grant, which previously was available broadly to support urban renewal and contribute to the supply of urban building land by reclaiming derelict sites. The national priorities have now been redefined to enable support to be given to the reclamation of sites both for development and environmental improvement. In rural areas, an emphasis is now placed on reclamation in areas of particularly high scenic quality. Government funding for the derelict land grant programme is £106 million in 1992–93.

New proposals to prevent land becoming derelict were announced in February 1992. Among these are:

—the wider use of conditions in planning permissions for certain industrial activities to oblige applicants to restore the land afterwards; and

—additional powers for local authorities to enable them to reclaim derelict land not in their ownership and seek a contribution to the cost from the owner.

Consultation is currently being carried out on these proposals.

Access to the Countryside

The Countryside Commission and its equivalents are the government bodies responsible for promoting access to the countryside (see p. 18). However, other measures are also important in helping the people of Britain to enjoy their natural heritage.

Footpaths and Other Rights of Way

There is a large network of rights of way in Britain, amounting to some 225,000 km (140,000 miles) in England and Wales alone. Of this length, some 76 per cent is made up of footpaths and another 20 per cent of bridleways. Highway authorities in England and

Wales,[5] and planning authorities in Scotland, are responsible for the maintenance of public footpaths, and for ensuring that rights of way are kept open.

Footpaths are sometimes obstructed or damaged. The Rights of Way Act 1990 allows farmers to disturb public paths but requires them to restore the surface rapidly. Following a major survey of the condition of rights of way in England and Wales, carried out in 1988, the Countryside Commission has set itself the goal of ensuring that the whole network in England is brought into good order by the year 2000, with the help of local authorities and landowners; the Government has endorsed this target. The CCW has initiated a scheme to bring a network of paths into good order by 1995.

Several long-distance paths, called national trails in England and Wales and long-distance routes in Scotland, have been designated, many of them along the coast. Together the 13 paths so far designated total some 3,400 km (2,100 miles). Proposals for a new national trail, the Thames Path, were approved in 1989; this is due to be opened in 1994. Smaller regional routes have also been established.

Land

There is no automatic right of access to open land in Britain. However, many landowners allow access more or less freely. Local planning authorities also have powers to secure access by means of agreement with landowners, and may acquire land or make orders for public access if such agreements cannot be reached. An example of such an access agreement was reached in 1990 between Bracknell Forest Borough Council and the Crown Estate. Under this, the

[5]In non-metropolitan areas, these are the county councils.

Crown Estate agreed to open up 1,200 hectares (3,000 acres) of land in Windsor Forest surrounding Bracknell's new heritage centre.

There are an estimated 600,000 hectares (1.5 million acres) of 'common land' in England and Wales; there is a legal right of public access to about one-fifth of this. Common land is usually in private hands, but people other than the owner have some rights over it, for example, for use as grazing land. Commons are protected by law and cannot be built on or enclosed without the consent of the Secretary of State for the Environment or for Wales.

The Government is working towards the provision of effective schemes of management to guarantee the conservation value of common land, and towards improved arrangements for public access. It will introduce legislation to these ends when parliamentary time permits. In Scotland, SNH is undertaking a major review of access to the countryside for recreation.

Forests

Britain was heavily wooded in prehistoric times, but most of the great forests have long since disappeared. However, the ecological, recreational and economic value of woodland is better recognised today. Woodland cover in Britain has risen from about 4 per cent of the land area in 1918 to about 10 per cent at present.

As part of this process, the Government has endorsed proposals for a new national forest in the Midlands. This will cover an area of almost 520 sq km (200 sq miles) where the boundaries of Derbyshire, Leicestershire and Warwickshire meet. This preferred area is the site of the ancient Needwood and Charnwood forests, and was chosen from a shortlist of five locations in the Midlands. Government funding of over £1 million is being made available through the Countryside Commission over three years to assist its development. The Forestry Commission and the Countryside Commission have jointly launched an initiative to create new 'community forests'. These are intended to be a mix of farmland, public open spaces and leisure facilities set in a well-wooded landscape. Consultation documents for the leading three forests—Thames Chase, east of London, the Mercia Forest in south Staffordshire and the Great North Forest in County Durham and Tyne and Wear—have recently been published. Another nine are planned, each covering 10,000 to 20,000 hectares (25,000 to 50,000 acres). Development teams for the national forest and the three lead community forests are currently drawing up business plans to set out in more detail how their objectives are to be achieved. The Government has also recently announced an initiative to revive Sherwood Forest in Nottinghamshire.

In Scotland, considerable progress has been made with the Central Scotland Woodlands Initiative. Some 6 million trees have already been planted in an area between Edinburgh and Glasgow through partnership between the Scottish Office, the Forestry Commission, local authorities, Local Enterprise Companies and the voluntary sector. Currently more than £1 million is being channelled through SNH in support of the project.

New planting by private owners is encouraged by means of the Woodland Grant Scheme. Grants are targeted to encourage an increasing amount of broadleaved planting, a shift in planting onto land of better quality, the planting of small woodlands and the maintenance of semi-natural woodlands. All planting schemes approved under the scheme are required to be in sympathy with the landscape and to meet relevant environmental considerations. Management grants were introduced in April 1992, with a higher rate for woodlands of special environmental importance. In addition, a community woodland supplement was introduced in February 1992 to assist in the implementation of the new forests and other smaller-scale initiatives. Opportunities for public access will be important to the award of such supplements.

The Government provided a package of assistance after a severe gale in October 1987 caused extensive damage to woodlands principally in south-east England. Its Task Force Trees has given grants totalling £11 million to replace some of the trees lost in 1987 and also in a further storm in January 1990.

Species Protection

Domestic Legislation

Rare and endangered species of native plants and animals are protected by law in Britain. The principal legislation under which this is done is the Wildlife and Countryside Act 1981, which applies to Great Britain. This provides specific protection for a number of animal species, as well as broad protection for wild birds, by making it an offence intentionally to kill, injure or disturb them. Rare plant species, too, are protected from intentional destruction or uprooting. Similar legislation applies in Northern Ireland.

The number of protected species has increased considerably in recent years. For example, in 1981 there were 62 fully-protected species of plant in Great Britain; by 1991 this had risen to 93. The number of fully-protected animal species rose from 47 to 89 over the same period. This does not include bird species; both in 1981 and 1991 all species occurring in Britain were fully protected except for 35 listed as partially protected. In addition, it is illegal to kill or injure certain species, while trade restrictions are imposed on others. The JNCC has a duty to review the list of protected species every five years and make recommendations for additions or deletions. The most recent review was completed in October 1991, and recommended that 18 animal and 73 plant species receive new or additional protection. The Government announced in July 1992 that an additional 87 species of plants and animals would be protected.

The Act also contains controls on the introduction of nonnative species. In February 1992 it was announced that, following consultation with the Government's nature conservation bodies, it had been decided to include an additional seven species of animals and several species of plants to the relevant schedule of the Act. This schedule previously contained 42 species of animals and four species of plants; it is illegal to release these or allow them to grow in the wild without a licence.

Species Management

Considerable research and management is carried out to encourage the recovery of populations of species threatened with extinction. The three nature conservation agencies have also set up recovery programmes for threatened species of plants and animals, such as the dormouse, the Plymouth pear and the fen raft spider. The aim is to ensure the survival of self-sustaining populations of these species in the wild.

Schemes can be devised to reintroduce species into areas where they have become extinct. For example, the red kite had died out in England and Scotland, although it was still found in Wales and Scandinavia. An international project was therefore co-ordinated by the JNCC and the Royal Society for the Protection of

Birds (RSPB—see p. 69) to bring adult birds from Sweden and, more recently, Spain and release them into the wild in areas where the species had become extinct. Other species that have been reintroduced in recent years include the white-tailed sea eagle and the large blue butterfly, both by the former Nature Conservancy Council. The Royal Botanic Gardens at Kew holds some 3,000 plant specimens which are extinct or under severe threat in the wild, and has had some success with reintroduction projects.

However, such schemes need to be carefully controlled. For example, measures to protect the barn owl were announced by the Government in February 1992. Since barn owl numbers have declined, principally due to loss of habitat, people have been breeding them in captivity and releasing them in the hope of boosting the wild population. However, many die within a short time, because some schemes give little thought to their needs once in the wild. The Department of the Environment therefore formed a working group with concerned organisations, and the Government has accepted the advice of this group. It announced its intention to make it illegal to release barn owls without a licence, to monitor licensed release schemes to assess their effectiveness, and issue guidance to increase awareness of the needs of barn owls and the difficulties involved in reintroduction schemes. The introduction of new measures for controlling the release of captive-bred barn owls was announced in November 1992.

International Trade

Indiscriminate trade in live or dead animals can threaten the survival of those species. Britain is a member of CITES (see p. 12), the international convention that controls trade in endangered species.

New measures to protect wild birds in trade were unveiled in February 1992 prior to a meeting of CITES. The Government announced that it would:

—press the International Air Transport Association to set world-wide limits on shipment sizes, failing which Britain would introduce its own stricter limits;

—introduce new checks on all imports into Britain of animals which may be threatened by trade;

—improve enforcement of existing transport conditions;

—apply stricter conditions to imports where appropriate;

—press for restrictions on trade in particular species between particular countries if numbers dying are excessive;

—press for worldwide bans on imports wherever there are sound scientific reasons for supposing that trade might be harmful to the survival of particular species populations; and

—introduce stricter requirements for the care and housing of live animals which may be threatened by trade.

Britain pledged an additional $1 million to elephant conservation in Africa at the CITES meeting in March 1992, to be spent in a number of countries following consultations as to how it might most effectively be used.

Research

The Government undertakes a considerable programme on environmental research, much of which is of benefit for conservation work. For example, in January 1992 the Government announced a research project into the rehabilitation of lowland bogs that have been affected by peat extraction. This aims to:

—assess the potential for rehabilitating worked-out and damaged peat bogs in Britain;

—assess the extent of retained flora and fauna necessary to facilitate rehabilitation through natural colonisation;

—provide the basis for guidance on appropriate working and reclamation methods; and

—identify gaps in current knowledge.

The project has an advisory steering committee, with representation from central and local government, the Peat Producers' Association, the JNCC, English Nature and voluntary conservation bodies.

Other research is aimed at the conservation of individual species or groups of species. For example, English Nature is currently carrying out a large research project investigating the ecology and habitat management requirements of the high brown fritillary, a rapidly declining species of butterfly.

Species Recording and Monitoring

Reliable information on the numbers and distribution of species is important in planning conservation strategies. Much research work is therefore done by conservation organisations to record and monitor animal populations. There are both national and local recording schemes, the latter usually collecting information on a county basis.

The most comprehensive data from monitoring mammal populations cover squirrels, red deer, otters and sea mammals. Seal populations are monitored by the NERC's Sea Mammal Research Unit by means of annual surveys of breeding grounds. The Forestry Commission carries out an annual survey of squirrels on

Major conservation and recreation areas

Orkney Islands

Shetland Islands

National Parks

Forest Parks

Areas of Outstanding Natural Beauty (National Scenic Areas in Scotland)

Heritage Coast (Coastal Conservation Zones in Scotland)

National Trails - - - - -

World Heritage Sites ◻

Speyside Way

S C O T L A N D

West Highland Way

Southern Upland Way

N O R T H E R N
I R E L A N D

Northumberland

North York Moors

Cleveland Way

Lake District

Wolds Way

Yorkshire Dales

Pennine Way

Peak District

Snowdonia

Offa's Dyke Path

Peddars Way and Norfolk Coast Path

The Broads (Special protected area)

W A L E S

E N G L A N D

Pembrokeshire Coast

Brecon Beacons

Pembrokeshire Coast Path

Ridgeway

North Downs Way

South Downs Way

Exmoor

Dartmoor

South West Coast Path

South West Coast Path

0   20   40   60   80   100 km

0   20   40   60 miles

The Giant's Causeway in Northern Ireland, an unusual formation of basalt rock formed into hexagonal pillars up to 6 m high, is included on the World Heritage List. Of Britain's entries on the list, it is the only naturally occurring feature.

Also on the World Heritage List are the castles and town walls of north Wales, built under Edward I. Conwy is shown here, with the castle's eight large towers at the right and the town, still surrounded by its walls, on the left. Also visible are Thomas Telford's crenellated suspension bridge and Robert Stephenson's tubular railway bridge.

Designation of land outside a town as Green Belt helps combat urban sprawl. The city of Oxford, seen here from nearby Boars Hill, is one of a number of towns and cities that have Green Belts.

Designations of sites in Britain under international agreements continue to be made. This site at Bala Lake in north Wales was designated in 1991—under the Ramsar Convention— as wetlands of international importance.

With a collection of 6 million preserved or dried specimens, the Royal Botanic Gardens at Kew, south-west London, perform valuable work in conserving rare species of plants. This example of a giant cycad from southern Africa is the world's oldest potted plant; the species is now threatened in the wild.

Marwell Zoo, near Winchester, is dedicated to the conservation of endangered species. Here a Siberian tiger displays one of her cubs, which was born at the zoo in October 1991.

The eighteenth century garden at Stowe, Buckinghamshire, features work by landscape designers such as William Kent and Capability Brown, and is now looked after by the National Trust. English Heritage has offered financial support of up to £311,000 to work such as these repairs to the Temple of Ancient Virtue.

This lake at Bosherton, Dyfed, was being affected by nutrient-rich water running off nearby farmland. Here a pipe is being laid to divert water to the lake's outflow.

The remains of the Rose Theatre (see p. 55) were discovered during redevelopment of the site. They are seen being covered up after archaeological examination for protection during building works. The new building, since completed, was redesigned so that the remains were not harmed and could be put on display later.

History comes alive at numerous events put on each year by English Heritage at many of the historic sites in its care. One of the groups that regularly appears is the Ermine Street Guard, who re-enact with great authenticity life in the Roman army.

Sometimes buildings no longer needed for their original purpose can be saved from demolition by conversion to new uses. Seen here is the former Hoover factory at Perivale in west London, a fine example of inter-war architecture, which has been adapted for a new lease of life as a Tesco superstore.

Liverpool Street station, in central London, is a fine piece of Victorian railway architecture. A recent award-winning project to regenerate and extend it has carefully preserved the character of the original; this shows the new grand entrance to the station.

Scotney Castle in Kent and its surrounding gardens are both in the care of the National Trust.

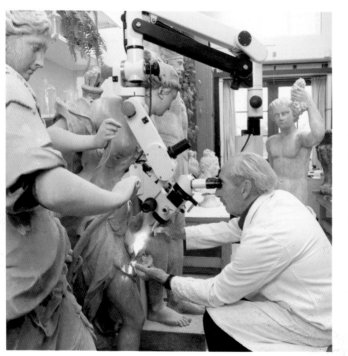

The National Trust can draw on the experience of many skilled workers. Here a conservation scientist examines statues brought from Cliveden House to a workshop in Maidenhead. The workshop, originally a department of the National Trust, is now financially independent.

its land; this has shown that the distribution of the red squirrel has declined in Wales and, to a lesser extent, in England over the past 20 years, but that it has remained at its higher level in Scotland. Surveys of otters in Great Britain have been carried out by the University of York over two periods (1977–79 and 1984–86); these found an increase in the number of river lengths that showed evidence of otter presence (see Table 2). They showed that otters are most common in Scotland and least so in England, although increases in distribution were greater in England and Wales than in Scotland.

Table 2: National Otter Surveys 1977–79 and 1984–86

	River stretches surveyed in both periods	Percentage of river stretches indicating otters present		% change
		1977–79	1984–86	
England	2,940	6	10	67
Wales	1,012	20	39	92
Scotland	2,650	57	65	14
Great Britain	6,602	29	36	27

Source: National Otter Survey/University of York.

Monitoring of bird populations is also carried out; indeed, it tends to be more intensive than for mammals. Organisations such as the RSPB and the British Trust for Ornithology assist in this. Table 3 shows summary results of bird monitoring in Britain, looking at species selected because there was sufficient data to be statistically valid.

Table 3: Summary of Monitoring Results of Selected Birds

	Period covered	Number of species examined	Population trends		
			Decr- ease	Little change	Incr- ease
Rare breeding birds	1973–89	25	4	10	11
Wildfowl	1960/1–89/90	19	1	4	14
Waders	1971–89	11	2	5	4

Sources: Rare Breeding Birds Panel; Wildfowl and Wetlands Trust; British Trust for Ornithology.

Another example of species monitoring is a JNCC scheme to monitor the abundance of butterflies. The scheme, which has been running since 1976, has shown very great changes in the abundance of certain species, often related to weather conditions. The scheme allows comparisons to be made between individual populations and national populations, and can give early warning of adverse changes.

The Built Heritage

Britain has a large number of old buildings, both grand and humble. Great efforts are made to preserve these for posterity, and to protect them both against neglect and modern development.

English Heritage

English Heritage, or the Historic Buildings and Monuments Commission, to give it its full title, protects England's heritage of historic buildings and monuments in several ways, including:

—managing some 400 historic properties (of which about 350 are open to the public) on behalf of the Secretary of State for National Heritage, including mansions, castles and ruined abbeys;

—giving grants for the repair of ancient monuments, historic buildings and buildings in 'conservation areas' (see p. 56);

—advising the Secretaries of State for the Environment and for National Heritage on their respective heritage casework, for example, on calling in applications for listed building consent and on the scheduling of ancient monuments; and

—advising local councils about applications to demolish or alter listed buildings.

It also organises a large number of events every year at the historic sites under its control, some 230 in the 1992 season. These vary from concerts and plays to recreations of historic events, and often involve the active participation of various clubs that have sprung up to re-enact history. The special events received an estimated 200,000 visitors, while its open-air concerts attracted 154,000 people.

English Heritage receives funding from the Government; in 1992–93 this will total some £102 million. However, it also gets money from other sources, such as admission charges to its sites, and membership fees from its 300,000 members. It employs a permanent staff of 1,600, including 400 curators, archaeologists and other conservation professionals.

In October 1992 English Heritage published its strategy for the 1990s. Its streamlining exercise would involve retaining care of the more important monuments and seeking to pass control of the less important ones to local management where possible. A programme of vigorous private sector fundraising is designed to widen support for key projects. Some of the powers inherited from the former Greater London Council could be dispensed with, following consultation with the London boroughs.

Wales and Scotland

The position within Wales and Scotland is slightly different. Two bodies—Cadw: Welsh Historic Monuments and Historic Scotland—have executive agency status within the Welsh and Scottish Offices. They parallel the activities of English Heritage and the built heritage responsibilities of the Department of National Heritage and the Department of the Environment, and manage about 125 and 330 monuments respectively. As with English Heritage, a wide range of different sites are protected—for example, one of the buildings cared for by Historic Scotland is the Dallas Dhu whisky distillery at Forres, Grampian, which was opened to the public in 1988.

Government Properties

A large number of historic buildings belong to the nation, and great efforts are made to keep them in good order. Current or recent projects include:

—a £30 million, ten-year refurbishment programme for the Foreign and Commonwealth Office building, Whitehall, designed by Sir George Gilbert Scott (1811–78);

—the repair of the Albert Memorial, South Kensington, also by Scott, to remedy the effects of water penetration and corrosion, which started in April 1990 and is expected to take about five years;

—the restoration of the south wing of Hampton Court Palace, devastated in a fire in March 1986; and

—an £8 million restoration of the 1840s Palm House at the Royal Botanic Gardens, Kew, completed in 1988.

At one time, the historic royal palaces of London—the Tower of London, Hampton Court, Kensington Palace, Kew Palace and the Banqueting Hall in Whitehall—were managed directly by the Department of the Environment. In October 1989, however, a new executive agency, the Historic Royal Palaces Agency, was set up to administer them. Responsibility for this transferred to the Department of National Heritage in April 1992. The Agency's aims include presenting the palaces and their history in a lively and attractive way. An example of this is the restoration of the old kitchens at Hampton Court to their original Tudor appearance.

The royal parks are also looked after by the Government; responsibility for those in England transferred from the Department of the Environment to the Department of National

Heritage in April 1992. Historic Scotland is responsible for looking after the Palace of Holyroodhouse and the royal parks in Scotland. An independent review group's recommendations on the restoration of the quality of London's royal parks was published in February 1992. Among other things, it recommended reintegrating Speakers' Corner in Hyde Park with Marble Arch. The report concluded that the impact of vehicle traffic on park users should be reduced greatly by such means as closing some roads in the parks. The traditional use of Hyde Park for royal and national celebrations should continue, but commercial events should be allowed only occasionally and when they are of benefit to the Park.

Royal Commission on the Historical Monuments of England

The Royal Commission on the Historical Monuments of England (RCHME), which was established in 1908, is responsible for documenting old buildings and structures in England. It is funded by the Government through the Department of National Heritage. Originally concerned with buildings pre-dating 1714, its remit has since been broadened to include material from the eighteenth and nineteenth centuries. Its most fundamental activity is compiling and maintaining the National Monuments Record, a public archive recording the architecture and archaeology of England. The RCHME has the right to make records of listed buildings (see p. 52) once consent has been given for their demolition or part-demolition; owners are obliged to give a month's notice of starting work and provide reasonable access. Similar commissions operate in Scotland and Wales.

Historic Churches

Britain has a very large number of historic churches and other religious buildings, many of them dating back to the Middle Ages. Because of their age, these are often expensive to maintain. Grants to help maintain small historic churches have been available for some years. However, in *This Common Inheritance*, the Government undertook to extend this assistance by establishing a cathedral repair grant scheme to help the upkeep of cathedrals and other comparable buildings. Details of this scheme, which is providing £11.5 million over three years, were announced in April 1991. The money is being channelled through English Heritage. However, the Government believes that this help should supplement rather than replace existing fund-raising and that public appeals and private donations should therefore continue to be the main source of funding. Cathedrals and other ecclesiastical buildings in Scotland were already eligible for help.

An Anglican church that is no longer needed for worship but is worth preserving can be transferred to the Redundant Churches Fund. The Fund, which was established in 1969, is financed both by the Government (which pays 70 per cent of its grant) and by the Church Commissioners, who pay the remaining 30 per cent. It currently cares for about 270 churches. The Government is considering whether to extend such help to religious buildings of other denominations. An independent charity, the Historic Churches Preservation Trust, also helps maintain old churches and chapels.

At present, church buildings in ecclesiastical use are exempted from listed building controls. However, the Government proposed in a consultation paper published in February 1992 that in future this exemption should be removed in respect of external works except in the case of ecclesiastical bodies which can show that their internal administrative systems include adequate controls over works to their historic churches. 'Ecclesiastical exemption' also applies in Scotland, although there are some minor differences in the way it works.

National Heritage Memorial Fund

The National Heritage Memorial Fund was set up under the National Heritage Act 1980 to assist with the preservation and maintenance of buildings, works of art, land and other items important for the national heritage. Non-profit-making bodies such as libraries and museums are eligible for its support. In 1991–92 the Fund helped the preservation of 88 heritage items ranging from historic houses to sculptures. The Government has increased the Fund's annual grant to £12 million. Although it does not normally help with repairs to historic buildings, in April 1990 the Fund made an exception by offering a grant of about £500,000 towards the restoration of the medieval Octagon and Lantern at Ely Cathedral. The Lantern is said to be the only true medieval timber dome in the world and is without parallel in British cathedrals.

Listed Buildings and Ancient Monuments

Both ancient monuments and important buildings are protected in law. There are a considerable number of such sites and buildings in Britain.

Listed Buildings

Buildings of special historic or architectural interest are 'listed' for statutory protection; the number of listed buildings has nearly doubled since the mid-1970s, as a systematic survey has led to more buildings being considered worthy of protection. The list is kept by the Government under provisions currently contained in the Planning (Listed Buildings and Conservation Areas) Act 1990. In Scotland, listing is done under the Town and Country Planning (Scotland) Act 1972, and in Northern Ireland under the Planning (Northern Ireland) Order 1991. In England and Wales, listed buildings are categorised with one of three grades: Grade I (the most important), Grade II* and Grade II. Similar categories of listing are used in Scotland and Northern Ireland.

Table 4: Scheduled Monuments and Listed Buildings

	Listed Buildings	Scheduled Monuments
England	440,000	13,000
Scotland	38,000	5,500
Wales	14,000	2,600
Northern Ireland	8,100	1,200

Sources: Department of the Environment, Scottish Office, Welsh Office, Department of the Environment for Northern Ireland.

All buildings built before 1700 which survive in anything like their original condition are listed, as are most of those built between 1700 and 1840. Fewer more recent buildings have been listed, but distinguished examples include the Willis Faber building in Ipswich, built in 1973–75 and listed Grade I in April 1991. Some of the structures that are listed are not even buildings in the ordinary sense of the word—for example, the Jodrell Bank radio telescope is listed, as are about 1,000 examples of the famous design of telephone kiosk by Sir Giles Gilbert Scott (1880–1960). Many London Underground stations, some of which are fine examples of inter-war architecture, are also listed. The Government has asked English Heritage to carry out research to identify examples of the main building types across the country and to provide guidelines for future listing. This research programme is scheduled to last three years. In Northern Ireland, the Government is committed to completing the survey and listing of pre-1914 buildings by 1993 and pre-1960 buildings by 1994. Thereafter listing will progress on the basis of a thirty-year rolling programme.

The decision to list a building is made by the relevant Secretary of State,[6] in Great Britain after taking advice from the heritage body concerned (English Heritage, Cadw or Historic Scotland). Surveys are done from time to time to see if any other buildings should be included. In addition, local planning authorities have the power to make a building preservation notice while its merits for listing are considered.

Once a building is listed, it enjoys a considerable degree of protection. It cannot be demolished without permission from the relevant local planning authority (in non-metropolitan parts of England and Wales, normally the district council). Before any alterations which affect its character are made, listed building consent must be obtained from the local planning authority, in addition to any planning permission that may be needed. Grants are available from English Heritage (or its equivalents) to assist owners of outstanding listed buildings who are otherwise unable to afford to keep them in reasonable repair. Powers are available to local planning authorities in certain circumstances to carry out urgent repairs to unoccupied listed buildings and to recover the cost of the work from the owner. An authority can also serve a repairs notice requiring the owner to carry out specified repairs for properly

[6] In England this is the Secretary of State for National Heritage, and in Wales, Scotland and Northern Ireland the respective territorial Secretary of State.

preserving the building. If these works are not carried out, the authority can begin proceedings compulsorily to purchase the building. Broadly similar powers apply in Scotland.

A recent report from English Heritage showed that most of England's listed buildings are in reasonable condition and that the vast majority are not at any risk. The report also showed that establishing alternative uses for old buildings could often be the key to their preservation.

Ancient Monuments

Ancient monuments of national importance can be 'scheduled' by the relevant Secretary of State—in England the Secretary of State for National Heritage—to receive legal protection. Broadly speaking, scheduled monuments rank in importance with Grade I or II* listed buildings. The term 'ancient monument' has a very wide meaning in Britain; it can include historic or architecturally important buildings in good repair or in ruins, or archaeological remains. For example, in February 1992 the remains of the sixteenth-century Rose Theatre in Southwark, south London, associated with William Shakespeare and rediscovered in 1989, were scheduled. The discovery took place during the construction of an office block, which was redesigned to preserve the remains and leave sufficient headroom for their possible future display. The Government agreed to pay up to £1 million to the developers to compensate them for their delay in building on the site. Now that the Rose remains have been scheduled, any future proposals for work, including those in connection with long-term preservation and possible display to the public, would have to be considered through the statutory scheduled monument procedures. Although many scheduled monuments in Britain are hundreds or even thousands of years old, scheduling is not confined to such sites. For example, East Fortune airfield in Lothian was scheduled in December 1990, as it was considered a rare survival of a wartime airfield with most of the buildings there intact and unaltered from their construction between 1938 and 1945.

As with listing a building, scheduling a monument confers protection on it, since any work to a scheduled monument can only be done with the Secretary of State's permission. English Heritage is currently engaged on a programme to evaluate all known archaeological remains in England and to identify those which may be suitable for scheduling. It is expected to result in a very significant increase in the number of scheduled monuments.

Conservation Areas

It can also be important to protect not only individual buildings but also the particular quality of an area. To help planning authorities do this, they are empowered to declare 'conservation areas'.

Conservation areas are districts of special architectural or historic interest whose character or appearance is such that it should be preserved and enhanced. A conservation area can be designated by a local planning authority, which has a duty to consider whether there are any areas within its boundaries that deserve this protection. The relevant Secretary of State also has the power to designate conservation areas. There are almost 8,000 conservation areas in England, more than 550 in Scotland, over 350 in Wales and 31 in Northern Ireland.

Once a conservation area has been designated, the local planning authority has to publish proposals for its preservation and enhancement. Stricter planning rules also apply. For example, some of the 'permitted development' rights[7] are removed. Any such development would now need planning permission. Planning applications that would affect the character of the area have to be advertised. Moreover, a stricter test than usual is applied when applications for such planning permission are decided: the council has to pay special attention to the desirability of preserving or enhancing the area. Demolition of houses within conservation areas is forbidden without 'conservation area consent', and the maximum penalties are considerable: up to two years' imprisonment, an unlimited fine, or both. Grants and loans are available from English Heritage for work that enhances the character of a conservation area. Again, similar arrangements apply in Scotland and Wales.

Another form of protection for an area of special character can be given by means of an 'article 4 direction'. This is provided for in article 4 of the General Development Order 1988, and has the effect of removing some or all permitted development rights from the properties concerned. Alterations specified in a direction, for example, the addition of satellite dishes, sun porches, double glazing and vehicle driveways—normally permitted development and which insensitively done can harm the appearance of a street or area—would then require specific planning permission. This gives the local planning authority means to control such changes.

Archaeology

Today's archaeological landscape is the product of human activity over thousands of years. It ranges through settlements and remains of every period and includes places of worship, defence

[7]Permitted development is the power to make alterations, generally minor, to a building without planning permission.

installations, burial grounds, farms and fields, and sites of manu-
facture. Archaeological remains are often highly vulnerable.

Scheduling as an ancient monument is an important mecha-
nism for safeguarding nationally important archaeological sites.
However, local authorities also play an important role, especially
through the planning system. Government guidance was issued by
the Department of the Environment in November 1990. This
stresses that the desirability of preserving ancient monuments
(scheduled or unscheduled), and their settings, must be taken into
account when planning applications are being decided.

Underwater archaeology is also important in a nation with a
strong maritime tradition. The conservation and proper study of
such sites was assisted in April 1991 by the transfer of responsibility for the protection of historic wrecks in English waters from the
Department of Transport to the Department of the Environment,
as promised in *This Common Inheritance*. Similar transfers took
place elsewhere in Britain. This brought together the control of
archaeology on land and under water. The Department of the
Environment's responsibility was transferred, together with that
for land archaeology, to the new Department for National Heritage
in April 1992. The RCHME has been given responsibility for the
preparation of a central record of historic wrecks. The Government
has also supported maritime archaeology by voluntary bodies, for
example, by giving the Nautical Archaeology Society a grant of
almost £30,000 in 1991–92 to develop its training programme.

Industrial, Transport and Maritime Heritage

Britain was the first country in the world to industrialise on a large
scale, and many advances in manufacturing and transport were
pioneered in Britain. This has resulted in a large industrial

heritage, the importance of which is being increasingly recognised. Important sites are scheduled or listed; one of the most important, the Ironbridge Gorge, where Abraham Darby (1677–1717) first smelted iron using coke, has been included on the World Heritage List (see p. 13). Other museums have also been set up, devoted to the preservation of industrial buildings and equipment.

As well as being protected for posterity, much of Britain's industrial heritage now gives pleasure to thousands of people today. A great deal of Britain's canal system survives in use, principally for pleasure craft. The publicly owned British Waterways Board (BWB) is responsible for some 3,200 km (2,000 miles) of waterways in Great Britain. It owns 60 tunnels, nearly 400 aqueducts, over 1,500 locks, 2,000 heritage structures and 57 SSSIs. In 1991–92 the BWB's turnover amounted to £77.9 million and it received a government grant of £49.7 million to maintain its waterways to statutory standards. Canal restoration programmes, often using volunteer help from societies such as the Inland Waterways Association, mean that more waterways are becoming available for such purposes. For example, in 1990 the BWB-owned Kennet and Avon Canal was reopened after being closed for almost 40 years, and in May 1991, 51 km (32 miles) of the privately owned Basingstoke Canal were reopened. These projects were largely financed by the local authorities through whose areas the canals pass, and they are contributing to their upkeep. An example of a major project being undertaken by the BWB is the repair of the Anderton Boat Lift, near Northwich in Cheshire, for which scheduled monument consent was given by the Government in July 1990. The lift, which linked the Trent and Mersey Canal with the River Weaver Navigation, was closed in 1984 after severe corrosion was found. A consortium of bodies has been founded to raise funds for this, including representatives from Cheshire County Council, the Inland Waterways Association, Northwich Town Council and the Trent and Mersey Canal Society. A full survey began in July 1991 in co-operation with English Heritage to see how much of the original structure can be retained.

Railways

Britain, which pioneered railways, has a fine heritage of railway buildings and structures, and there is an active movement to preserve it. Volunteers are very active in this. A large number of disused railway lines have been bought by railway preservation societies and returned to operation, often using preserved steam locomotives, and several railway museums have been established. The Association of Railway Preservation Societies, a co-ordinating body for the railway preservation movement, lists over 150 corporate members and many individual members. The work of such bodies is sometimes assisted by government grants and projects. For example, in 1991–92 the East Lancashire Railway received about £300,000 in derelict land grant to acquire the route of a former railway, and has received approval in principle of up to £1.25 million more aid to restore it to railway use. Also contributing to the conservation of Britain's historic railways is the Railway Heritage Trust. This independent company, set up in 1985, is supported by British Rail and offers grant aid for the preservation of listed railway buildings and structures. It helps the British Rail Property Board preserve non-operational buildings and structures with a view to their transfer to other bodies.

Shipping

Important reminders of Britain's maritime past are also preserved. The historic naval dockyard at Chatham has been opened to the public; at Portsmouth HMS *Victory*, Nelson's flagship, HMS

Warrior, the world's first iron battleship and the remains of *Mary Rose*, raised from the seabed in 1982, are open to the public. The Imperial War Museum has preserved the cruiser HMS *Belfast*, which is open to the public in the Pool of London. Isambard Kingdom Brunel's SS *Great Britain*, the world's first large screw-driven ship, is preserved in Bristol. A voluntary body, the Maritime Trust, has been established to preserve vessels and other maritime things of historic or technical interest. The Trust's vessels open to the public include the clipper *Cutty Sark* at Greenwich.

Improving the Environment

As well as protecting Britain's cities and towns, a great deal of work is being done to improve the quality of the local environment. The Government gives help to inner city areas through the Urban Programme. This is spent for a variety of different purposes, many directed towards improving the local economy. However, projects designed to improve the quality of the environment are also helped.

The Voluntary Sector

Voluntary organisations also play a vital role in conservation. Some groups protect the natural environment or wildlife, others look after Britain's built heritage. The largest of the voluntary groups working for conservation in Britain is the National Trust, which protects both countryside and historic buildings. The Government assists the work of the voluntary sector by providing considerable financial support for it. The multiplicity of conservation groups is such that only a summary can be given here of the voluntary sector conservation work in Britain.

Participation

Voluntary groups vary considerably in the number of members they attract, but some are very large. Table 5 shows recent membership figures for certain of them. It also shows how some of these organisations have expanded their membership considerably in recent years.

Some groups exist to help people to get physically involved in conservation work. For example, the British Trust for Conservation Volunteers (BTCV) organises over 400 'working holidays' every year, as well as putting on courses in practical skills. The RSNC's (see p. 70) 55,000 volunteers work over 500,000 days a year.

The National Trust

The National Trust for Places of Historic Interest or Natural Beauty, to give it its full name, is an independent charity that owns

Table 5: Membership of Voluntary Bodies

	1971	1981	*Thousands* 1990
National Trust	278	1,046	2,032
Royal Society for the Protection of Birds[a]	98	441	844
Civic Trust[b]	214	–	302
Royal Society for Nature Conservation[c]	64	143	250
National Trust for Scotland	37	110	218
Ramblers' Association	22	37	81
Council for the Protection of Rural England	21	29	44

Source: *Social Trends.*

[a] Including members of the Young Ornithologists' Club.
[b] Members of local amenity societies registered with the Civic Trust.
[c] Not including members in junior organisations.

and protects areas of landscape and historic buildings. It was set up in 1895, and has since grown to over 2 million members. It operates throughout Britain, except in Scotland, where there is a separate National Trust for Scotland. It remains independent of the Government, although it accepts state help in the form of grants in the same way as other owners of important buildings.

Countryside

A key original aim of the Trust was to protect open country from development for the benefit of the people of Britain, at a time before the development of government planning policies to combat urban sprawl. It now owns about 230,000 hectares (570,000 acres), as well as having legal agreements to protect another 30,000 hectares (75,000 acres). Its properties include 160 gardens, 59 villages, woodlands, nature reserves and antiquities such as a significant length of Hadrian's Wall. Some of the Trust's properties are used as country parks.

Enterprise Neptune

A 1963 survey showed that about a third of Britain's coast was outstandingly beautiful and worth preserving. Enterprise Neptune, the Trust's campaign to protect the coastline, was therefore launched in 1965. It aimed to:

—acquire and preserve fine coastline;

—focus public attention on the problem of coastal development; and

—improve the quality of the Trust's existing coastline by good management.

At that time, 300 km (185 miles) of coastline in England, Wales and Northern Ireland were in the protection of the Trust. Subsequently, more than £17 million has been raised and the amount of coastline protected by the Trust has risen to 853 km (530 miles).

Historic Buildings

The Trust was not set up primarily to protect historic buildings. However, by the 1930s the future of many great houses was being threatened by the increasing cost of upkeep. An Act of Parliament was therefore passed in 1937 to allow the Trust to hold investments to provide money for the upkeep of property. By the end of the 1940s, 36 houses had come into the care of the Trust. When accepting a house, the Trust also requires an 'endowment' to support it, since the income from entrance fees will usually not cover the cost of maintenance. The Trust's policy is not to acquire buildings unless they are in danger of harm if they remain in private hands. It must also be assured that the public will benefit, not just from the preservation of a building but also from access to it.

Support from both the public and private sectors is sought to acquire and preserve country houses. For example, in 1985 the Government accepted Calke Abbey in Derbyshire in lieu of tax. The house was offered to the Trust, which needed £7.4 million for urgent repairs and as an endowment. The money was raised from a variety of sources—the National Heritage Memorial Fund, English Heritage, the district council, the trustees of the Harpur-Crewe estate (the previous owners) and a public appeal. After restoration, the house opened to the public, and attracted 106,000 visitors in 1990.

Conservation is an important part of the Trust's work, not least because of the large numbers of visitors to many of its houses. To minimise the wear and tear caused, many preventative measures are taken, but repair work is also needed. The most up-to-date conservation techniques are used, mostly by freelance conservators. A severe test of the Trust's restoration skills was posed by a devastating fire at Uppark House in Hampshire in 1989; the house will be reopened after major repairs.

Public Access

Public access to the Trust's property is a very important part of its land management policies. Some 10.7 million people were recorded as visiting the Trust's properties in 1991, besides those who enjoyed free access to the countryside and coasts owned by the Trust. However, there needs to be a balance between preservation and access, so that too many visitors do not damage the sites they come to visit. The Trust takes various steps to protect its properties from excessive numbers of people. For example, at some houses 'timed tickets' have been introduced. These allow access at a particular time, and visitors can look around the grounds while they are waiting. The size of car park can also be used: at many properties the Trust has built car parks large enough for most occasions but which will deter visitors at peak periods. There are also restrictions on visitors at some of the most important wildlife habitats.

Organisation and Finance

The Trust's policy is set by its council. Half the council members are elected by the members of the Trust, and the other half are appointed as representatives of other conservation groups. The Trust is run from day to day by its staff, based in London and in its regional offices. It employs about 2,400 people permanently.

The Trust obtains its income from various sources. About half comes in membership fees, gifts and legacies. Other sources of money include sales from shops at the properties, renting out holiday cottages and running events. Special appeals are made to raise money for particular properties or activities in need of extra assistance.

National Trust for Scotland

There is a separate National Trust for Scotland, founded in 1931. Its aims and conservation policies are broadly similar to those of the National Trust in the rest of Britain. It has in its care over 100 properties and over 40,000 hectares (100,000 acres) of land. The wide range of properties reflects the history and social development of Scotland; as well as large houses, there are also simple town houses and cottages, and examples of Scotland's industrial heritage. The Trust owns the sites of Bannockburn (1314) and Culloden (1746), two of the most important battles in Scottish history. Several of Scotland's islands are in the Trust's care, including Staffa, Canna and most of Iona. The St Kilda islands are leased to SNH because of their wildlife, but the Trust organises volunteer working parties to restore their now-deserted buildings.

Membership is almost 235,000; over 2 million people visited the Trust's properties in 1991. The Trust, like its counterpart, has a policy-making council consisting partly of elected members and partly of members representing other interested Scottish groups. There is an executive committee to oversee the day-to-day running of the Trust. Its staff consists of about 300 people, rising to about 700 in the summer season.

A particular emphasis of the National Trust for Scotland is the protection of the domestic architecture of towns and villages. Under its 'Little Houses Improvement Scheme', houses are bought, restored and then sold with safeguards to protect them from future alteration. Money from the sale is then used to repeat the process elsewhere. The scheme was launched in 1960; by the beginning of 1990, 243 buildings had been repaired under the scheme.

Natural Heritage Groups

Britain has a great number of other voluntary organisations aimed at the protection of its natural heritage. These groups carry out a wide range of different activities. For example, some campaign for changes in the law or government policy, some maintain nature reserves and others organise volunteers for work sessions at different sites.

Countryside Protection

Council for the Protection of Rural England
The Council for the Protection of Rural England, which was founded in 1926, seeks to protect the rural landscape from intrusions such as motorways and airports. It campaigns on many countryside issues, such as water pollution, farming methods and planning controls over farm buildings. At a local level, its 44 county branches seek to influence planning and development control. Its parallel organisations, the Campaign for the Protection of Rural Wales, the Association for the Protection of Rural Scotland and the Ulster Society for the Preservation of the Countryside, share similar aims.

Farming and Wildlife Advisory Group
The Farming and Wildlife Advisory Group is a registered charity based at the National Agricultural Centre in Warwickshire. There are currently 65 county groups affiliated to the national organisation in all parts of Britain. It works in partnership with many other conservation groups and bodies, such as the Countryside Commission, the Forestry Commission, English Nature and the RSPB. It seeks to stimulate the management of an attractive, living countryside which can benefit everyone. It encourages the integration of economically sound farming with environmentally responsible methods of production. There are currently 41 farm conservation advisers working with the county groups, all of whom

have a sound knowledge both of agriculture and conservation; in 1990–91 they visited almost 2,700 farms. A closely-linked Scottish organisation is responsible for 16 Scottish groups.

Ramblers' Association

The Ramblers' Association aims to protect the interests of all who walk in the countryside, especially by defending the public path network, securing access to mountains and moorlands, and by preserving the landscape which visitors to the countryside enjoy.

Open Spaces Society

The Open Spaces Society campaigns to protect commons, village greens, rights of way and other open spaces in town and countryside. It produces a wide range of publications on these topics and offers advice to local authorities, commons committees and voluntary organisations.

Woodland Trust

The Woodland Trust is a national charity whose aim is to safeguard trees and woodland by raising funds to buy and look after woods that might otherwise be destroyed. It also plants young trees to create woods for the future. It is one of Britain's largest non-commercial woodland owners and has raised over £13 million for conservation purposes.

Wildlife

Royal Society for the Protection of Birds

The RSPB, founded in 1889, is one of the largest wildlife societies in the world. Its Young Ornithologists Club, with over 116,000 members, is the largest club of its kind in the world. The RSPB aims to maintain Britain's heritage of wild birds and increase it where desirable. It conducts research into birds and their habitats and campaigns on issues related to the conservation of birdlife, for example, the trade in wild-caught birds. It owns or manages 118 reserves totalling some 77,000 hectares (190,000 acres), including 5 per cent of Britain's estuaries. As well as maintaining reserves in Britain, it also supports bird conservation overseas. Other work of the RSPB included help for the International Council for Bird Preservation to send specialists to Saudi Arabia and Kuwait to assess the damage to birdlife caused by the release of oil into the Gulf by the Iraqis during the war in early 1991.

Royal Society for Nature Conservation

The Royal Society for Nature Conservation (RSNC) is an umbrella organisation comprising 47 local nature conservation trusts, owning or managing over 2,000 nature reserves totalling more than 52,000 hectares (128,000 acres). A new three-year pilot scheme was launched by English Nature in May 1992 to help voluntary bodies by meeting up to half the cost of managing their nature reserves; initially it is the RSNC county wildlife trusts that will be eligible for this support.

Scottish Wildlife Trust

The Scottish Wildlife Trust, which is affiliated to the RSNC, seeks to protect wildlife in Scotland by creating and managing nature reserves, encouraging public interest in conservation, providing education facilities, and advising landowners and users as to how their activities might best benefit wildlife. It currently manages 83 reserves covering some 18,000 hectares (44,500 acres).

Wildfowl and Wetlands Trust

The Wildfowl and Wetlands Trust maintains eight national wild-fowl centres in Britain, the most famous being at Slimbridge in Gloucestershire. This 355-hectare (880-acre) site is the world's largest and most varied wildfowl reserve. The Trust aims to conserve wildfowl and their wetland habitat and to help the public to a greater appreciation of wildfowl as part of the natural heritage. Its work is not confined to Britain; successes abroad include the reintroduction of Hawaiian geese to the Hawaiian Islands and the increase of the Spitsbergen flock of barnacle geese from 400 to over 12,000. The Trust has some 60,000 members.

World Wide Fund for Nature

The World Wide Fund for Nature (WWF) was formed in 1961 to raise money for the conservation of wildlife and natural habitats everywhere; it is the largest voluntary international nature conservation body in the world. WWF-UK is one of the largest and most active of its 27 national and associate organisations. Of the money it raises, one-third is spent on conservation projects throughout Britain and two-thirds is channelled into overseas projects, mainly in developing countries. WWF helps support the purchase of threatened sites to secure their future and campaigns on environmental issues. It has a large education programme aimed at both children and adults.

The Built Environment

There are also a great number of organisations that aim to protect and enhance ancient monuments and buildings of architectural interest, and improve the built environment.

Civic Trust

The Civic Trust and its equivalent, the Scottish Civic Trust, were established to uphold high standards of environmental quality and management in Britain. The Civic Trust receives government help for some of its work but is principally dependent upon public support in the form of sponsorship, donations and membership subscriptions. Among the Trust's activities are:

—making annual awards for development and restoration work which enhances its surroundings;

—providing advice and assistance in urban regeneration;

—providing a forum for all those involved in environmental education to come together; and

—supporting a network of 1,000 local amenity societies registered with the Trust.

The Civic Trust has built up a substantial amount of expertise in its field, and so can deal with the hundreds of enquiries that it receives every week. An example of the work of the Civic Trust is the *Building a Better Britain '92* exhibition, which took place in May 1992 at the Business Design Centre in London. Over 100 displays were mounted at the exhibition from architects, contractors, developers and building material producers, showing how careful design and construction could enhance the environment. Another example is the Loftus project, helped by English Heritage and the RDC. This aims to regenerate the town of Loftus in Cleveland, which had been gradually declining for some years.

The Scottish Civic Trust is similar in its aims and structure; like its equivalent, it relies mainly on voluntary sources of income, with a measure of government support. Like the Architectural

Heritage Society of Scotland, it plays a formal role in listed building and scheduled monument consent cases in Scotland.

Building Preservation Groups

There are a number of groups seeking to protect old buildings, some fairly broad in their scope, and others that campaign to foster interest in the architecture of particular periods and to preserve buildings from that period.

Ancient Monuments Society

The Ancient Monuments Society, founded in 1924, is a national body concerned with the conservation and preservation from unjustified demolition of historic buildings of all periods, styles and types throughout Britain. It must be consulted statutorily on any application to demolish a listed building. The Society maintains historic buildings directly through its partnership with the Friends of Friendless Churches. It also runs an educational programme encompassing lectures, study-tours, and publication of newsletters and transactions.

Save Britain's Heritage

Save Britain's Heritage—Save for short—was founded in 1975 to campaign publicly for the preservation of historic buildings, as well as campaigning on broader issues of conservation policy. It emphasises the possibilities of finding alternative uses for historic buildings that are no longer needed for their original purpose, and in a number of cases has prepared its own schemes for the re-use of threatened properties. Save has established two charitable trusts to restore two particular buildings, Barlaston Hall in Staffordshire and All Souls Church in Halifax. It has produced many publications on historic buildings.

Society for the Protection of Ancient Buildings

The Society seeks to ensure the preservation and care of buildings of historic or architectural interest. By law, it must be consulted on applications to demolish listed buildings. It is able to give technical advice, and provides scholarships enabling students to study old buildings and means of repairing them. It also maintains a register of houses threatened with demolition.

Georgian Group

The Georgian Group exists to protect Georgian buildings, monuments and parks from destruction. It seeks to stimulate public interest in Georgian architecture, town planning and artistic taste and to promote the appreciation of the classical tradition. It was founded in 1937 in response to the demolition of many of London's eighteenth-century buildings between the wars, at a time before the introduction of the present system of listing buildings of merit. As well as its work in seeking to protect Georgian buildings, it also runs a programme of activities for its members. It must be consulted statutorily on applications to demolish listed buildings.

Victorian Society

Founded in 1958, the Victorian Society is a national group that studies and campaigns to protect Victorian and Edwardian architecture and other arts. It has several regional branches. The Society is primarily a pressure group seeking to avoid the needless demolition or unsuitable alteration of buildings of interest. It must be consulted on applications to demolish listed buildings, and often gives evidence at planning inquiries. Linley Sambourne House in Kensington, west London, is run by the Society as a museum. This building has survived largely unchanged as an example of a late Victorian interior. The Society organises a programme of lectures, conferences and other events.

Twentieth-Century Society

The Twentieth-Century Society, which until May 1992 was known as the Thirties Society, campaigns broadly for the protection of buildings built after 1914 and seeks to create public interest in inter-war architecture. It advises local authorities on planning applications that affect buildings erected after the First World War.

Council for British Archaeology

Founded in 1944, the Council for British Archaeology exists to advance the study and practice of archaeology in Great Britain, and to promote the education of the public in British archaeology. Archaeology is taken to include all aspects of the built historic environment, and the Council must be consulted statutorily on applications to demolish listed buildings.

Groundwork Foundation

Important in the work of improving the built environment is the Groundwork organisation. The Groundwork Foundation, established in 1985, works in partnership with public bodies, the private sector and voluntary organisations to promote the care and enhancement of the urban environment and its rural fringes. This work is carried out through a network of local Groundwork Trusts. More than 3,000 environmental projects have been completed throughout England and Wales over a five-year period. During the 1980s, over 3,000 organisations and 50 local authorities partnered Groundwork.

Special projects include the New Countryside Initiative, an expert partnership including Groundwork, the Ministry of Agriculture, Fisheries and Food, and the Countryside Commission. It aims to explore the opportunities arising from changes in agricultural practices and land use to:

—create greater prosperity for edge-of-town farmers;

—improve relationships between farmers and their urban neighbours; and

—create a better countryside.

Tidy Britain Group

The Tidy Britain Group is a voluntary organisation that encourages environmental improvements and the reduction of litter, both in cities and also in the countryside. It received a government grant of £1.8 million in 1991–92. It organises campaigns and seminars on litter abatement in both urban and rural surroundings. A neighbourhood litter watch scheme was launched in 1990.

UK 2000

UK 2000 was launched in 1986 as a partnership between government, voluntary organisations, industry and local authorities; Government grant in 1991–92 was £1.9 million. It aims to improve the environment and bring economic regeneration. The founder members include:

—the British Trust for Conservation Volunteers (see p. 62);

—the Civic Trust;

—Community Service Volunteers;

—Friends of the Earth;

—the Groundwork Foundation; and

—the RSNC.

Environment Wales

A review of UK 2000 and the Special Grants Programme was undertaken in 1990. As a result, a new initiative, Environment Wales, was launched in March 1992 with a budget of £500,000. It aims to develop a strategic approach to environmental projects, encourage partnerships and, as far as possible, create a strong and self-sustaining voluntary sector.

Government Support

The Government supports voluntary organisations' work to improve and enhance the environment, often with conservation-related projects. In 1992–93, assistance from the Environmental Grant Fund will total almost £1 million to 49 separate groups. The activities of groups assisted include canal restoration in various areas, the provision of advice on environmental aspects of mineral extraction, monitoring dolphin and porpoise populations around English coasts, advice on building conservation, and local conservation projects run by RSNC member trusts.

The Government is introducing a new fund, the Environmental Action Fund, in 1993–94. It will assist voluntary organisations carrying out environmental work and has been established to rationalise the Department of the Environment's support for environmental work in this sector. Almost £4 million will be available in the Fund for 1993–94.

In 1992–93 the Government is also assisting 16 groups running projects contributing to urban improvement and regeneration under the Department of the Environment's Special Grants Programme; this aid will total more than £430,000. Support of £385,000 is also being made available to 21 voluntary organisations carrying out heritage work. Groups assisted include the Ancient Monuments Society, the Georgian Group, and the Victorian Society. Help is also being given towards groups promoting industrial and maritime archaeology. In addition, in 1992–93 nearly £31.2 million was offered to 40 organisations working in the environmental protection and countryside fields under the Special Grants Programme. In Scotland, the Special Grants (Environmental) Programme will distribute £323,000 in 1992–93, assisting 39 organisations with central administration costs and supporting upwards of 12 projects designed to further the environmental aims set out in *This Common Inheritance*. UK 2000 Scotland will receive £408,000 to pay for development staff and projects.

Addresses

Government Departments and Agencies

Department of the Environment, 2 Marsham Street, London SW1P 3EB.

Department of the Environment for Northern Ireland, Parliament Buildings, Stormont Castle, Belfast BT4 3SS.

Department of National Heritage, Government Offices, Horse Guards Road, London SW1P 3AL.

Scottish Office, New St Andrew's House, Edinburgh EH1 3SZ.

Welsh Office, Cathays Park, Cardiff CF1 3NQ.

Cadw: Welsh Historic Monuments, Brunel House, 2 Fitzalan Road, Cardiff CF2 1UY.

Countryside Commission, John Dower House, Crescent Place, Cheltenham, Gloucestershire GL50 3RA.

Countryside Council for Wales, Plas Penrhos, Ffordd Penrhos, Bangor, Gwynedd LL57 2LQ.

English Heritage, Fortress House, 23 Savile Row, London W1X 1AB.

English Nature, Northminster House, Peterborough PE1 1UA.

Forestry Commission, 231 Corstorphine Road, Edinburgh EH12 7AT.

Historic Scotland, 20 Brandon Street, Edinburgh EH3 5RA.

Joint Nature Conservation Committee, Monkstone House, City Road, Peterborough PE1 1JY.

National Heritage Memorial Fund, 10 St James's Street, London SW1A 1EF.

Natural Environment Research Council, Polaris House, North Star Avenue, Swindon, Wiltshire SN2 1EU.

Royal Commission on the Ancient and Historical Monuments of Scotland, 16 Bernard Terrace, Edinburgh EH8 9NX.

Royal Commission on the Ancient Monuments of Wales, Crown Buildings, Plas Crug, Aberystwyth, Dyfed SY23 2HP.

Royal Commission on the Historical Monuments of England, Fortress House, 23 Savile Row, London W1X 1AB.

Rural Development Commission, 11 Cowley Street, London SW1P 3NA.

Scottish Natural Heritage, 12 Hope Terrace, Edinburgh EH9 2AS.

Voluntary Organisations

Ancient Monuments Society, St Ann's Vestry Hall, 2 Church Entry, London EC4V 5HB.

Architectural Heritage Society of Scotland, The Glasite Meeting House, 33 Barony Street, Edinburgh EH3 6NX.

Association for the Protection of Rural Scotland, Gladstone's Land, 3rd Floor, 483 Lawnmarket, Edinburgh EH1 2NP.

Association of Railway Preservation Societies, 3 Orchard Close, Watford, Hertfordshire WD1 3DU.

British Trust for Conservation Volunteers, 36 St Mary's Street, Wallingford, Oxfordshire OX10 0EU.

Buildings at Risk Trust, 1 Greenhill, Wirksworth, Derbyshire DE4 4EN.

Campaign for the Protection of Rural Wales, Ty Gwyn, 31 High Street, Welshpool SY21 7JP.

Civic Trust, 17 Carlton House Terrace, London SW1Y 5AW.

Council for British Archaeology, 112 Kennington Road, London SE11 6RE.

Council for the Protection of Rural England, Warwick House, 25 Buckingham Palace Road, London SW1W 0PP.

Farming and Wildlife Advisory Group, National Agricultural Centre, Stoneleigh, Kenilworth, Warwickshire CV8 2RX.

Georgian Group, 37 Spital Square, London E1 6DY.

Groundwork Foundation, 85-87 Cornwall Street, Birmingham B3 3BY.

Inland Waterways Association, 114 Regent's Park Road, London NW1 8UQ.

Maritime Trust, 2 Greenwich Church Street, London SE10 9BG.

National Trust, 36 Queen Anne's Gate, London SW1H 9AS.

National Trust for Scotland, 5 Charlotte Square, Edinburgh EH2 4DU.

Open Spaces Society, 25a Bell Street, Henley-on-Thames, Oxfordshire RG9 2BA.

Railway Heritage Trust, Melton House, 65 Clarendon Road, Watford, Hertfordshire WD1 1DP.

Ramblers' Association, 1-5 Wandsworth Road, London SW8 2XX.

Redundant Churches Fund, 89 Fleet Street, London EC4Y 1DH.

Royal Society for Nature Conservation, The Green, Witham Park, Waterside South, Lincoln LN5 7JR.

Royal Society for the Protection of Birds, The Lodge, Sandy, Bedfordshire SG19 2DL.

Save Britain's Heritage, 68 Battersea High Street, London SW11 3HX.

Scottish Civic Trust, 24 George Square, Glasgow, G2 1EF.

Scottish Wildlife Trust, Cramond House, Cramond Glebe Road, Edinburgh EH4 6NS.

Society for the Protection of Ancient Buildings, 37 Spital Square, London E1 6DY.

Tidy Britain Group, The Pier, Wigan, Greater Manchester WN3 4EX.

Twentieth-Century Society, 58 Crescent Lane, London SW4 9PU.

UK 2000 Scotland, c/o Scottish Power, 201 Drakemire Drive, Glasgow G45 9TD.

Victorian Society, 1 Priory Gardens, Bedford Park, London W4 1TT.

Woodland Trust, Autumn Park, Grantham, Lincolnshire NG31 6LL.

Wildfowl and Wetlands Trust, Slimbridge Centre, Slimbridge, Gloucestershire GL2 7BT.

World Wide Fund for Nature UK, Panda House, Weyside Park, Godalming, Surrey GU7 1XR.

Further Reading

			£
Action for the Countryside.	Department of the Environment	1992	Free
Action for Rural Enterprise.	Rural Development Commission	1991	Free
Countryside Stewardship: an Outline. CCP 346.	Countryside Commission	1991	Free
Environment in Trust.	Department of the Environment	1991	Free
Environmental Directory. ISBN 1 870257 057.	Civic Trust	1988	4.00
Green Rights and Responsibilities in Scotland: a Citizen's Guide to the Environment.	Scottish Office	1992	Free
This Common Inheritance: Britain's Environmental Strategy. Cm 1200. ISBN 0 10 112002 8.	HMSO	1990	27.00
This Common Inheritance: the First Year Report. Cm 1655. ISBN 1 10 116552 8.	HMSO	1991	21.00
This Common Inheritance: the Second Year Report. Cm 2068. ISBN 0 10 120682 8.	HMSO	1992	21.00
The Environment and the British Aid Programme.	ODA	1990	Free

Annual Statistics

The UK Environment.	HMSO
Digest of Environmental Protection and Water Statistics.	HMSO
The Scottish Environment Statistics.	Scottish Office
Environmental Digest for Wales.	Welsh Office

Acronyms and Abbreviations

AONBs	Areas of Outstanding Natural Beauty
BTCV	British Trust for Conservation Volunteers
BWB	British Waterways Board
CITES	Convention on International Trade in Endangered Species of Wild Fauna and Flora
CCS	Countryside Commission for Scotland
CCW	Countryside Council for Wales
ESAs	Environmentally Sensitive Areas
HMIP	Her Majesty's Inspectorate of Pollution
IPC	Integrated pollution control
IWC	International Whaling Commission
JNCC	Joint Nature Conservation Committee
MNRs	Marine nature reserves
NNRs	National nature reserves
NRA	National Rivers Authority
NSAs	National scenic areas (Scotland)
NERC	Natural Environment Research Council
NHAs	Natural heritage areas (Scotland)
NCC	Nature Conservancy Council
NCCS	Nature Conservancy Council for Scotland
RCHME	Royal Commission on the Historic Monuments of England
RSNC	Royal Society for Nature Conservation
RSPB	Royal Society for the Protection of Birds
RDC	Rural Development Commission
SNH	Scottish Natural Heritage
SSSIs	Sites of Special Scientific Interest
WWF	World Wide Fund for Nature

Index

Printed in the UK for HMSO.
Dd 0295920, 1/93, C30, 512423, 5673.

CURRENT AFFAIRS:
A MONTHLY SURVEY

Using the latest authoritative information from official and other sources, *Current Affairs* is an invaluable digest of important developments in all areas of British affairs. Focusing on policy initiatives and other topical issues, its factual approach makes it the ideal companion for *Britain Handbook* and *Aspects of Britain*. Separate sections deal with governmental; international; economic; and social, cultural and environmental affairs. A further section provides details of recent documentary sources for these areas. There is also a twice-yearly index.

Annual subscription including index and postage £35·80 net.
Binder £4·95.

Buyers of Britain 1993: An Official Handbook *qualify for a discount of 25 per cent on a year's subscription to* Current Affairs *(see next page).*

HMSO Publications Centre
(Mail and telephone orders only)
PO Box 276
LONDON SW8 5DT
Telephone orders: 071 873 9090

THE ANNUAL PICTURE

BRITAIN HANDBOOK

The annual picture of Britain is provided by *Britain: An Official Handbook* - the forty-fourth edition will be published early in 1993. It is the unrivalled reference book about Britain, packed with information and statistics on every facet of British life.

With a circulation of over 20,000 worldwide, it is essential for libraries, educational institutions, business organisations and individuals needing easy access to reliable and up-to-date information, and is supported in this role by its sister publication, *Current Affairs: A Monthly Survey*.

Approx. 500 pages; 24 pages of colour illustrations; 16 maps; diagrams and tables throughout the text; and a statistical section. Price £19·50.

Buyers of Britain 1993: An Official Handbook *have the opportunity of a year's subscription to* Current Affairs *at 25 per cent off the published price of £35·80. They will also have the option of renewing their subscription next year at the same discount. Details in each copy of* Handbook, *from HMSO Publications Centre and at HMSO bookshops (see back of title page).*